5
KINDS OF
NONFICTION

5 KINDS OF NONFICTION

Enriching Reading and Writing Instruction with Children's Books

Melissa Stewart
Marlene Correia

Routledge
Taylor & Francis Group

NEW YORK AND LONDON

A Stenhouse Book

First published 2021 by Stenhouse Publishers

Published 2024 by Routledge
605 Third Avenue, New York, NY 10017
4 Park Square, Milton Park, Abingdon, Oxon OX14 4RN

Routledge is an imprint of the Taylor & Francis Group, an informa business

Library of Congress Cataloging-in-Publication Data

Names: Stewart, Melissa, author. | Correia, Marlene P., author.
Title: 5 kinds of nonfiction: enriching reading and writing instruction
   with children's books / Melissa Stewart and Marlene Correia.
Other titles: Five kinds of nonfiction
Description: Portsmouth, New Hampshire : Stenhouse Publishers, [2021] |
   Includes bibliographical references and index. |
Identifiers: LCCN 2020009854 | ISBN
   9781625314178 (paperback)
Subjects: LCSH: English language—Composition and exercises—Study and teaching
   (Elementary) | Children's books. | School children—Books and reading.
Classification: LCC LB1576 .S7964 2020 | DDC
   372.6/044—dc23
LC record available at https://lccn.loc.gov/2020009854

Cover design by Cindy Butler
Interior design and typesetting by Gina Poirier, Gina Poirier Design

ISBN 13: 978-1-62531-417-8 (pbk)
ISBN 13: 978-1-03-268043-9 (ebk)

DOI: 10.4324/9781032680439

To the many educators who have supported and contributed to my nonfiction advocacy, especially Alyson Beecher, Lesley Burnap, Mary Ann Cappiello, Michele Knott, Judi Paradis, Melanie Roy, Terrell Young, and Terrence Young. —M.S.

To teachers who spark a love of literacy by never giving up the quest to discover the right book, for the right child, at the right time. —M.C.

Text Permissions

Portions of this book were adapted from the following sources:

Bukowiecki, E., and M. Correia. 2017. *Informational Texts in Pre-kindergarten Through Grade-Three Classrooms*. Lanham, MD: Rowman & Littlefield. Used by permission of Rowman & Littlefield.

Stewart, M. 2015, December 21. "Diversity in Thinking." A Fuse #8 Production/*School Library Journal*. Retrieved from *http://blogs.slj.com/afuse8production/2015/12/21/guest-post-melissa-stewart-and-diversity-in-thinking/*. Used by permission of Elizabeth Bird and *School Library Journal*.

Stewart, M. 2016, Fall. "What the Heck Is an Informational Book?" *The SCBWI Bulletin*, 21–22. Used by permission of the Society of Children's Book Writers and Illustrators.

Stewart, M. 2017, September 21. "A Look at Expository Literature." A Fuse #8 Production/*School Library Journal*. Retrieved from *http://blogs.slj.com/afuse8production/2017/09/21/guest-post-melissa-stewart-a-look-at-expository-literature/*. Used by permission of Elizabeth Bird and *School Library Journal*.

———. 2018, May. "The Five Kinds of Nonfiction." *School Library Journal*, 12–13. Used by permission of *School Library Journal*.

———. 2020, August. "Expository vs. Narrative Nonfiction." *School Library Journal*, 16. Used by permission of *School Library Journal*.

———. 2020, Fall. "Voice in Nonfiction Writing," *The SCBWI Bulletin*, 19–21. Used by permission of the Society of Children's Book Writers and Illustrators.

Stewart, M., and T. A. Young. 2018. "Defining and Describing Expository Literature." In *Does Nonfiction Equate Truth? Rethinking Disciplinary Boundaries Through Critical Literacies*, ed. V. Yenika-Agbaw, R. M. Lowery, and L. A. Hudock (11–24). Lanham, MD: Rowman & Littlefield. Used by permission of Rowman & Littlefield.

———. 2019. "Teaching the Key Traits of Expository Nonfiction with Children's Books." *The Reading Teacher* 72 (5): 648–651. Used by permission of John Wiley and Sons.

CONTENTS

Acknowledgments xii

Notes from the Authors xiv

Understanding Nonfiction: An Overview 1

CHAPTER 1

How Nonfiction Got Its Name 2

What *Exactly* Is Informational Text? 3

Two Nonfiction Writing Styles 5

Introducing the 5 Kinds of Nonfiction 10

CHAPTER 2

A New Nonfiction Classification System 11

Traditional Nonfiction 13

Browseable Nonfiction 14

Narrative Nonfiction 16

Expository Literature 17

Active Nonfiction 19

Looking Ahead 20

Why Students Need Access to a Diverse Array of Nonfiction 22

CHAPTER 3

What Kinds of Books Do You Prefer? 23

What Kinds of Books Do Most Educators Prefer? ... 23

What Kind of Books Do Children Prefer? 27

What Kind of Books Do Your Students Prefer? ... 28

Expository Nonfiction in the Classroom 31

Rethinking Your Book Collection 37

CHAPTER 4

How Understanding the 5 Kinds of Nonfiction Helps Readers and Writers ... 39

Teaching the 5 Kinds of Nonfiction to Students 40
Applying the 5 Kinds of Nonfiction 44
A Deeper Dive into Nonfiction Craft 56

CHAPTER 5

Using the 5 Kinds of Nonfiction to Explore Text Patterns 61

Patterns in Fiction and Nonfiction 62
The Power of Patterns: Text Features 62
The Power of Patterns: Text Format 65
The Power of Patterns: Interruption Construction ... 72
The Power of Patterns: Text Scaffolding 75

CHAPTER 6

Using the 5 Kinds of Nonfiction to Explore Text Structures 78

Text Structures in Reading 79
Text Structures in Writing 86

CHAPTER 7

Using the 5 Kinds of Nonfiction to Explore Voice, Language, and Point of View 95

Commercial Nonfiction vs. Literary Nonfiction 96
The Voice Choice 99
Language Matters 103
What's Your Point of View? 107

CHAPTER 8

Sharing the 5 Kinds of Nonfiction with Students 117

Introducing Nonfiction Books 118
Celebrating Nonfiction Books 124
Evaluating Nonfiction Books 132

What's the End Game?

What's the End Game? **137**

What Is Blended Nonfiction? 138
What Is Gateway Nonfiction? 141
The Critical Role of Blended Nonfiction
    in Literacy Development 143

APPENDIX A Obtaining the Children's Books
    in This Guide 145

APPENDIX B Resources for Finding
    High-Quality Nonfiction 146

APPENDIX C Activity Planner 147

APPENDIX D Reproducibles for Activities 152

APPENDIX E Nonfiction Picture Books That
    Are Perfect for Reading Aloud 157

Bibliography of Children's Books 160
Professional References 177
Book Cover Permissions 188
Index 214

Acknowledgments

We gratefully acknowledge Colby Sharp for inviting Melissa to make the video that introduced the Nerdy Book Club community to the 5 Kinds of Nonfiction classification system and Valerie Bang-Jensen, Vickie Blankenship, Tom Bober, Abi Diaz, Kristen Picone, Melissa Pillot, Carole Stubeck, and Jen Vincent for being early adopters. We appreciate their willingness to do the book-sorting activities with their students and collect data about student preferences.

We would also like to thank children's book authors Sarah Albee, Brenda Z. Guiberson, Steve Jenkins, Jess Keating, and Sara Levine for agreeing to be interviewed and educators Tom Bober, Abi Diaz, Valerie Glueck, Traci Kirkland, Ruth McKoy Lowery, Shelley Moody, Kristen Picone, Jen Vincent, and Terrence Young for providing quotations that appear in the book; children's book authors Loree Griffins Burns and Heather Montgomery and retired school librarians Karen Kosko and Terrence Young for taking the time to read the manuscript and offer valuable suggestions; Valerie Bang-Jensen, Karen Blumenthal, and Kate Narita for offering sage advice at just the right moments; and Gerard Fairley for his assistance in securing permissions and preparing the back matter.

A special thank-you to the many educators and friends who took photos and supplied student work samples for the book, including Vickie Blankenship, Sarah S. Brannen, Catherine Burns, Ann Davis, Robin DeCosta, Jason Lewis, Kathleen Merten, Shelley Moody, Kendall Newman, Melissa Pillot, Alyssa Pimentel, Katelyn Rebello, Mary Shorey, Stacey Snyder, Donna Sullivan-McDonald, Maria Sylvain, Ann Williams, and Judy Williams. An extra shout-out to Michele Knott who supplied seventeen images!

Thank you to Terry Thompson for encouraging us to write this book and offering exemplary editorial support through the process. We are also grateful to the entire Stenhouse staff, including Shannon St. Peter, Stephanie Levy, Cindy Butler, Gina Poirier, Pamela Hunt, and

Cindy Black. And finally we would like to extend a heartfelt thank-you to all the children's book authors, illustrators, and publishers (Bloomsbury; Boyds Mills Press & Kane; Candlewick; Capstone; Charlesbridge; Chicago Review Press; Chronicle; HarperCollins; Holiday House; Houghton Mifflin Harcourt; Lerner; Little, Brown; Macmillan; National Geographic; Peachtree; Penguin Random House; Rosen; Scholastic; Simon & Schuster; Sterling; Storey; Two Lions; and What on Earth? Books) who gave us permission to use the cover images of their books free of charge.

A Note from Melissa

There aren't many children's book authors who have written close to 200 nonfiction books and not a single fiction title, so it's no surprise that one of the most common questions children ask me during school visits is if I'll ever write fiction. For years, I gave the same answer every single time: "Maybe, I just need to find the right story."

I don't know if that answer satisfied the students, but it certainly didn't satisfy me because it was a lie. You see, in my professional life, I'm surrounded by people who prize stories and storytelling, and, for a long time, I thought I should too.

I remember praising the format of a particular picture book biography during a presentation at a writing conference in Texas. Later, a friend who is a celebrated children's book author kindly pointed out that, to her, the characters in that book seemed a bit wooden. That comment, and others like it from authors, editors, and educators I respect, gradually made me realize that I don't experience stories in the same way as my colleagues. I felt like an oddball, like I was all alone in a world that valued narratives.

But then in 2014, I was doing a weeklong residency at a small school in Maine. By the last day, I was really getting to know the students, and I felt comfortable with them. So when a fourth grader asked THE question, I finally decided to be honest.

I asked the group: "How many of you like to write fiction?" Many hands went up, as I knew they would. Then I took a deep breath and said, "I know lots of writers who love to create characters and invent imaginary worlds. But for me, the *real* world is so amazing, so fascinating, that I just want to learn as much as I can about it and share it with other people. That's why I write nonfiction."

And then something astonishing happened. A boy in the back row—a child none of the teachers expected to participate—lifted his arm, extended his pinky and his thumb, and enthusiastically rocked his hand back and forth. A half dozen other students joined him.

"Me too," they were saying. "We agree."

I had validated their way of thinking, their experience in the world, and they were validating me right back. It was a powerful moment.

I now know that those students are what Ron Jobe and Mary Dayton-Sakari call "info kids." While many educators think of non-fiction, especially expository nonfiction, as broccoli, info kids think differently. To them, expository text on topics that interest them is like chocolate cake.

My hope is that *5 Kinds of Nonfiction: Enriching Reading and Writing Instruction with Children's Books* will help educators gain a deeper understanding of all that today's nonfiction has to offer, so that they can stock their bookshelves and enhance their instruction with the kinds of books that all students find delicious.

Melissa Stewart

A Note from Marlene

At a professional development workshop I attended around 2005, the presenter asked us to list all the texts we had recently read. As I jotted down my responses—a recipe, emails, a professional journal, the newspaper—I came to the sudden realization that even though most of what I read as an adult was nonfiction, the bookshelves in my kindergarten classroom were full of fictional picture books. In fact, I couldn't recall the last time I had read aloud a nonfiction book to

my students. I began to wonder—did that matter? Even though I was confident that my students were more interested in fiction, my curiosity was piqued.

That was the inspiration for an action research study that changed my attitude toward nonfiction forever. For nineteen weeks, I tracked my kindergarten students' library book choices and recorded the number of fiction versus nonfiction books checked out.

I asked the school librarian for help in selecting quality nonfiction books that were appropriate for my kindergarten students and matched their interests. After adding the titles she recommended to my classroom collection, I watched to see how often those books were in students' hands. I also began reading nonfiction aloud and noticed that the children were captivated. They requested books about famous athletes, their favorite pets, butterflies, dangerous bugs, sports, and even ballet.

At the end of the action research study, it was clearly evident that the children had proved my initial thinking wrong. As a group, they checked out more nonfiction than fiction fourteen out of the nineteen weeks. After reviewing the numbers and informally observing book selection in my newly (almost) balanced classroom collection, I was convinced that the children enjoyed reading nonfiction texts.

After completing that initial study, I have repeated it on some scale with other groups of students in various grade levels and settings. Each time, the outcome is similar. Reflecting on my work with this action research, I am thankful that student choices, discussion, and my observations compelled me to change my thinking and my teaching practices.

If someone asked me today to list all the texts I've read recently, I can assure you it would still include emails and journal articles and the digital newspaper, but I'm proud to say that it would also include some nonfiction books that I've read for pleasure. It's my hope that *5 Kinds of Nonfiction: Enriching Reading and Writing Instruction with Children's Books* will help teachers realize the potential of nonfiction to deepen student learning, fuel their interests, and cultivate their curiosity about the world around them.

Marlene Correia

1

Understanding Nonfiction: An Overview

"*I like nonfiction because you gain knowledge.
Then you ask more questions.*"

—Asher, fourth grader

How Nonfiction Got Its Name

In most schools, children are taught the difference between fiction and nonfiction in kindergarten. Ask any first or second grader to explain the two terms, and about half will proudly say, "Fiction is fake, and nonfiction is real." This answer may lack nuance, but it gets the job done.

But some students get flustered by this question. They find it difficult to distinguish between two words that sound so similar, and it's no surprise. It truly is confusing to define a word by what it isn't.

To uncover the story behind the term "nonfiction" and how books bursting with ideas and information got saddled with such a negative name, we need to travel back in time to 1876. That's when American librarian and educator Melvil Dewey invented an ingenious book-cataloging system that was quickly adopted by libraries around the world (Comaromi 1976). But the Dewey Decimal System wasn't perfect. By the early 1900s, a growing number of library patrons were complaining that it was difficult to find "a good story." That's because novels and short story collections were interspersed among all the other categories of literature (essays, letters, speeches, satire, etc.) in the 800s. And because all the books in the 800s were organized by original language of publication, novels by American writers were nowhere near novels by German writers or French writers.

How did librarians solve this problem? Sometime between 1905 and 1910, they started pulling novels and short story collections out of the 800s and creating a separate "fiction" section with books arranged alphabetically by the author's last name (Paradis 2015, Schiesman 2016). At that time, the term *fiction* was defined as "literature comprising novels and short stories based on imagined scenes or characters" (*Online Entomology Dictionary ND*). It traces back to the Old French word *ficcion*, which

---

TEACHING **TIP**

In many school libraries, librarians have rearranged their nonfiction sections in ways that help students find books more easily. They have created separate sections for biographies, folktales and folklore, and poetry. And in some collections, books about rockets (629) are now shelved with books about planets and other space objects (520-525), while books about Egyptian mummies (930) and non-Egyptian mummies (390) now sit side by side on bookshelves. This is a trend we think will continue.

meant "dissimulation, ruse; invention, fabrication"—basically the definition most early elementary students give today.

Not long after separating fiction from the rest of the collection, librarians began calling everything left behind (still arranged according to Dewey's system) *nonfiction* (Paradis 2015, Schiesman 2016). Besides factual books based on documented research, the nonfiction section included drama, poetry, and folktales.

What *Exactly* Is Informational Text?

Eventually, librarians realized that they needed a term to describe just the factual, research-based books in their nonfiction collections. Around 1970, they began calling these titles *informational books* (Schiesman 2016). That's why the Robert F. Sibert Informational Book Medal, which is sponsored by the American Library Association, defines *informational books* as "those written and illustrated to present, organize, and interpret documentable, factual material" (Association for Library Service for Children 2015).

Patricia Newman (l), author of the 2018 Sibert Honor title *Sea Otter Heroes: The Predators That Saved an Ecosystem*, with Sibert committee chair Tali Balas

Unaware of what was happening in the 1980s, literacy educators defined *informational books* as a narrow subset of nonfiction writing that presents information about science, history, and other content areas (Pappas 1986, 1987). According to this usage, *informational books* do not include biographies, how-to books, or any kind of narrative writing.

For a while, librarians and educators used their separate definitions with few problems. But when the U.S. Congress passed the No Child Left Behind Act of 2001, schools changed their funding priorities, and school library budgets started to shrink. To save their jobs, school librarians began taking on new roles, including teaching responsibilities (Paradis 2015). Not surprisingly, this led to confusion about the proper use of the term *informational books*.

The misunderstanding increased in 2010 when the Common Core State Standards defined *informational text* in a much broader way, including all narrative and expository nonfiction books (the librarian definition) plus reference books, instructions, forms, maps, persuasive essays, and so on (NGAC and CCSSO 2010). As a result, we now have three contradictory definitions floating around.

Because the term "informational book/informational text" doesn't have a standard, universal definition, for the sake of precision we avoid using it as much as possible in our teaching lives and in this book. However, because many schools have an "informational writing" unit in their curriculum, we do use that term when we discuss instructional strategies related to that unit of study.

What *Exactly* Is Informational Fiction?

The term *informational fiction* refers to books that contain a significant amount of true information that's supported by documented research but also have some made-up parts. These books include historical fiction, like the Dear America series and picture book biographies with some invented dialogue, imagined scenes, or events presented out of chronological order to improve the storytelling. They also include STEM-themed books that present concepts accurately but contain made-up characters, fantastical art, or other embellishments. Examples include The Magic School Bus series, books narrated by animals or inanimate objects, and some animal life cycle stories.

This helpful term acknowledges that, in some cases, taking creative liberties with true, documentable facts can be an effective way to share ideas and information with young readers. But it also emphasizes the importance of distinguishing between what's real, what's true, what's verifiable, and what's not.

Two Nonfiction Writing Styles

As we discussed the competing definitions of "informational book/ informational text" in the previous section, we introduced two important terms—*narrative nonfiction* and *expository nonfiction*. If you're like most educators, you've probably heard these terms, but you might not be completely clear about the difference between these two writing styles.

Let's start with what narrative nonfiction and expository nonfiction have in common. They're both meticulously researched, and every single fact and idea the author includes can be verified.

The difference between the two writing styles lies in *how* the ideas and information are presented, as shown in Figure 1.1. Narrative nonfiction tells a story or conveys an experience, whereas expository nonfiction explains, describes, or informs in a clear, accessible fashion.

Narrative nonfiction appeals strongly to fiction lovers because it includes real characters and settings, narrative scenes, and, ideally, a

FIGURE 1.1 Two Writing Styles

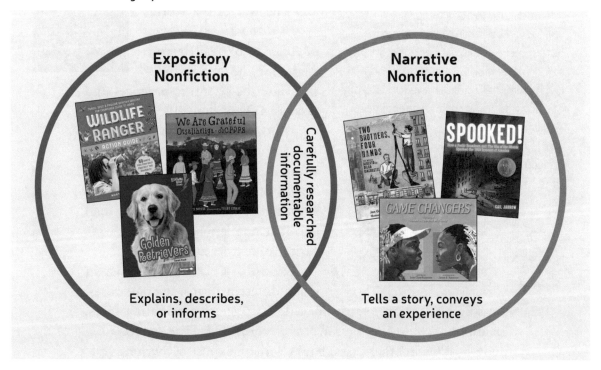

narrative arc with rising tension, a climax, and a resolution (Aronson 2016). The scenes, which give readers an intimate look at the world and people being described, are linked by expository bridges that provide necessary background while speeding through parts of the true story that don't require close inspection (Fleming 2015).

The art of crafting narrative nonfiction lies in pacing, which means choosing just the right scenes to flesh out. Narrative nonfiction typically features a Chronological Sequence text structure and is ideally suited for biographies, such as *Game Changers: The Story of Venus and Serena Williams* by Lesa Cline-Ransome and *Two Brothers, Four Hands* by Jan Greenberg and Sandra Jordan. It also works especially well for books that recount historical events, such as *Spooked! How a Radio Broadcast and* The War of the Worlds *Sparked the 1938 Invasion of America* by Gail Jarrow. And it may be used in books that describe scientific practices and processes (May et al. 2019).

Book Bonanza!

Throughout this book, we recommend lots of children's books your students will love. If you aren't sure how to obtain these books, Appendix A offers some suggestions. To identify more great children's books in the future, you can use the resources in Appendix B. You can also go to www.routledge .com/9781625314178 or scan the QR code to view periodic updates of key book lists in *5 Kinds of Nonfiction*.

Expository nonfiction shares ideas and information in a more direct, straightforward way. It often relies heavily on art and design to help convey meaning, and it's more likely than narrative nonfiction to include a wide variety of text features.

Expository nonfiction comes in many different forms. In some cases, the sole goal of an expository title is to share fascinating facts. Examples include *Guinness World Records* and *Time for Kids Big Book of Why*. In other cases, books with an expository writing style

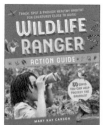

can help readers learn a new skill, such as baking cookies or making origami. *Wildlife Ranger Action Guide: Track, Spot & Provide Healthy Habitat for Creatures Close to Home* by Mary Kay Carson describes how to locate, identify, and protect local wildlife.

Some expository nonfiction books provide a general overview of a topic, such as the human body or Ancient Egypt. *Golden Retrievers* by Sarah Frank shares all kinds of information about the popular dogs.

Expository nonfiction can also focus on a specific concept, such as how our skeleton is similar to those of other animals or unusual ways birds use their feathers. *We Are Grateful: Otsaliheliga* by Traci Sorell takes an in-depth look at how the Cherokee community expresses gratitude and celebrates its way of life all through the year. These more specialized books often present ideas and information in creative or unexpected ways.

ACTIVITY 1.1

Comparing Narrative and Expository Nonfiction

One of the best ways for you and your students to gain a solid understanding of the difference between narrative and expository writing styles is to read

and compare the books *Red-Eyed Tree Frog* by Joy Cowley (narrative) and *Frog or Toad? How Do You Know?* by Melissa Stewart (expository). These books are short and simple, and they're both about frogs.

As you read *Red-Eyed Tree Frog*, you can easily identify all the elements of a good story.

> ### TEACHING **TIP**
>
> Suggested grade levels for all the activities in this book are listed in Appendix C. Feel free to modify them to meet the specific needs of your students.

Pages 2–3   Author introduces setting (evening in the
             rain forest)

Pages 4–5   Author introduces main character (the
             red-eyed tree frog)

Pages 6–7   Author introduces main conflict (the frog is
             hungry)

Pages 8–9   Frog searches for food

Pages 10–11 Frog searches for food

Pages 12–13 Author introduces subconflict (a hunting boa
             constrictor)

Pages 14–15 Rising tension (snake moves toward frog)

Pages 16–17 Rising tension (snake spots frog)

Pages 18–19 Resolution of subconflict (frog jumps to
             safety)

Pages 20–21 Frog spots a moth

Pages 22–23 Resolution of main conflict (frog eats moth)

Pages 24–25 Falling action (frog climbs onto leaf)

Pages 26–27 Falling action (frog goes to sleep)

Pages 28–29 Satisfying circular ending (morning comes to
             rain forest)

Before you begin reading *Frog or Toad? How Do You Know?*, take a few minutes to preview this expository nonfiction book in search of text features. You will find a table of contents (page 2), glossary (page 3), list of references (pages 22–23), and index (page 24). As you page through the main text, you will notice headings, photos with labels, and boldface glossary terms.

As you read, you will see that the book is organized as follows:

Pages 4–5   Introduction

Pages 6–7   Compares skin of frog (verso) to the skin of
             the toad (recto)

Pages 8–9   Compares length of back legs of frog (verso) to length of back legs of toad (recto)

Pages 10–11   Compares body shape of frog (verso) to body shape of toad (recto)

Pages 12–13   Compares teeth of frog (verso) to teeth of toad (recto)

Pages 14–15   Compares song of frog (verso) to song of toad (recto)

At this point, stop reading for a moment and ask a question: What is the book's text structure? Even elementary readers who have recently been introduced to text structures can easily answer this question. It's Compare & Contrast.

Now flip to the end of the main text and examine the colorful double-page infographic. It provides a fitting conclusion by summarizing all the frog vs. toad characteristics described throughout the book.

By reading these books aloud and discussing them, both adults and students can gain a solid understanding of the key differences between narrative nonfiction and expository nonfiction writing styles.

Now that you've read Chapter 1, you have a solid understanding of what nonfiction is—and what it isn't. You've also learned to distinguish between the two nonfiction writing styles (narrative and expository). This foundation will serve you well as you forge ahead to Chapter 2. We're excited to introduce you to the 5 Kinds of Nonfiction—a useful new system for classifying nonfiction children's books based on how they present information and how they can be used most effectively in a school setting.

CHAPTER 2

Introducing the 5 Kinds of Nonfiction

"The 5 Kinds of Nonfiction classification system brings clarity to the way we think about nonfiction. We're used to subdividing our fiction section into genres like mysteries and science fiction. But then we just lump all the nonfiction together. Now we can see smart, useful ways to categorize these books too."

—Traci Kirkland, librarian, Boyer Elementary School, Prosper, Texas

A New Nonfiction Classification System

You may not remember reading or learning about narrative nonfiction when you were in school. That's because until fairly recently there was really only one kind of nonfiction for children—survey (all-about) books that use concise, straightforward expository language to provide a general overview of a topic. Popular examples include titles written by such authors as Gail Gibbons and Seymour Simon.

While traditional survey books are still being published, they're no longer the only option young readers have. In the last twenty-five years, nonfiction children's books have changed tremendously, developing in new and exciting ways. Despite these changes, most teachers continue to think about and organize their classroom nonfiction collections in the same way as teachers working twenty, thirty, even forty years ago—by topic. Contrast this with the way most teachers think about and organize their fiction titles.

Most educators recognize that some young readers love a good mystery. Other children prefer science fiction, fantasy, or adventure stories. To help students find books they love, most classroom book collections group fiction titles by genre. The books in a given genre have easily recognizable characteristics that appeal to some young readers more than others. We'd like to encourage teachers to consider the benefits of classifying nonfiction in a similar way.

Classroom Library vs. Classroom Book Collection

Research shows that access to a full-time, state-certified school librarian improves student test scores, closes the achievement gap, and improves writing skills (Kachel and Lance 2013). And yet, due to budget cuts and misunderstandings about the critical role libraries play in a school community, only 61.9 percent of U.S. elementary schools have a full-time school librarian (Tuck and Holmes 2016). Clearly, school libraries and the dedicated librarians who run them need our support.

One way to do that is by acknowledging the difference between the collection of books teachers keep in their classroom for students to read independently and a carefully curated library maintained by a trained certified school librarian. To highlight that distinction, we are *not* using the term "classroom library" in this book. Instead, we use "classroom collection" and "classroom book collection," terms that are preferred by the school librarian community.

As the children's nonfiction market has expanded and innovated in recent years, books have evolved into the five distinct categories shown in Figure 2.1. Understanding the characteristics of these categories can help young readers predict the type of information they're likely to find in a book and how that information will be presented. And once students are equipped with those skills, they can quickly and easily identify the best books for a particular purpose as well as the kinds of nonfiction books they enjoy reading most. We'll discuss these important benefits in greater detail in Chapter 4.

FIGURE 2.1 5 Kinds of Nonfiction

Four of the five categories of nonfiction children's books have an expository writing style.

The 5 Kinds of Nonfiction classification system is the outcome of Melissa's desire to better understand the wide world of nonfiction books for children. In 2012, she began her effort by developing a nonfiction family tree that included various categories and attempted to highlight how they were related to one another. She published a few different versions of the family tree on her blog, but none of them seemed quite right.

Then, in 2013, Melissa learned that a group of highly respected educators who called themselves the Uncommon Corps had developed a nonfiction taxonomy (Stewart 2013). She was fascinated by their ideas. Although the group's classification system never caught on, Melissa began an ongoing dialogue with several members. Marc Aronson, Sue

Bartle, Mary Ann Cappiello, and Myra Zarnowski have all influenced the way she thinks about nonfiction.

Over the next four years, Melissa continued to refine her thinking, and by December 2017, her family tree seemed truly useful. When she posted it on her blog, the response was tremendous. Teachers, librarians, children's book authors, and editors all loved the idea of classifying nonfiction into five categories—active nonfiction, browseable nonfiction, traditional nonfiction, expository literature, and narrative nonfiction. People praised the clarity the classification system brought to the range of children's nonfiction available today.

Eventually, Melissa realized that a tree model wasn't the most effective way to represent her ideas, and she began referring to her classification system as the 5 Kinds of Nonfiction. We hope that after reading this book, you'll find it as useful as we do.

The rest of this chapter focuses on describing the 5 Kinds of Nonfiction being published today and provides recently published sample books. By evaluating and comparing a selection of these titles, you'll develop a stronger sense of how they can be classified and how understanding the characteristics of the categories can inform your work with students.

Traditional Nonfiction

Thanks to the invention of desktop publishing software, which has transformed the page makeup process, traditional nonfiction survey books—the kind you probably remember reading as a child—are more visually appealing than they were in the past.

At one time, these books were text heavy with just a few scattered black-and-white images that decorated the pages rather than

We Need Inclusive Nonfiction!

While we're excited to see a recent uptick in narrative nonfiction by and about Black, Indigenous, and People of Color (BIPOC), there are currently very few children's books with an expository writing style by authors and illustrators from traditionally underrepresented and marginalized groups. Because we hope this will change soon, we'll be periodically updating many of our book lists online at www.routledge.com /9781625314178, so that we can feature more inclusive titles in all five nonfiction categories.

enriching the content and meaning. But today, traditional nonfiction often has a more dynamic design with an abundance of colorful, captivating photos, which are integral to the presentation. These books, which are often published in large series, continue to emphasize balance and breadth of coverage and include language that's clear, concise, and straightforward (Hepler 1998; Kiefer 2010). They typically employ a Description text structure and have an expository writing style.

Traditional nonfiction is ideal for the early stages of the research process, when students are "reading around" a topic to find a focus for their report or project. The straightforward, age-appropriate explanations make the information easy to digest, which is helpful to students who are just beginning to learn how to synthesize and summarize information as they take notes.

Here are six recently published examples:

Behind the Scenes Gymnastics by Blythe Lawrence

Coral Reefs by Gail Gibbons

Exoplanets by Seymour Simon

Golden Retrievers by Sarah Frank

Monster Trucks by Matt Doeden

Rivers and Streams by Cathryn Sills

Browseable Nonfiction

In the late 1980s, Dorling Kindersley's innovative Eyewitness Books series brought remarkable changes to expository nonfiction for young readers (Lodge 1996). These beautifully designed, lavishly illustrated books with short text blocks and extended captions revolutionized children's nonfiction by giving fact-loving kids a fresh, engaging way to access information. Readers can easily dip in and out of browseable books, focusing on the sections that interest them most, or they can read the books cover to cover (Emmett 2012). Today, many companies publish fact-tastic books in this category, and kids love them.

Due to their wide array of text features, browseable books are well suited for the later stages of the research process, when students are seeking specific information and looking for tantalizing tidbits to engage their audience of readers.

Here are six recently published examples:

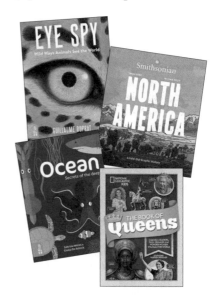

Big Book of WHY Revised and Updated by Editors of Time for Kids

The Book of Queens by Stephanie Warren Drimmer

Eye Spy: Wild Ways Animals See the World by Guillaume Duprat

Guinness World Records 2019 by Guinness World Records

North America: A Fold-Out Graphic History by Sarah Albee

Ocean: Secrets of the Deep by Sabrina Weiss and Giulia De Amicis

What's in a Name?

In 2012, Jennifer Emmett, senior vice president at National Geographic for Kids, introduced Melissa to the term "browseable books" at a Society of Children's Book Writers and Illustrators nonfiction writing retreat in Silver Bay, New York. It was the perfect label for books inspired by Dorling Kindersley's Eyewitness Book series.

Narrative Nonfiction

Developed in the 1960s and 1970s by such celebrated adult authors as Truman Capote and Norman Mailer, narrative nonfiction first appeared in children's titles in the mid-1990s. This style of writing, which we discussed in detail on pages 5–9, slowly gained momentum over the next two decades. Today, it's the writing style of choice for biographies and books that focus on historical events. It also works well for books that describe processes, such as natural cycles or how scientists carry out investigations.

Because narrative nonfiction titles often lack headings and other text features, they aren't as useful for targeted research as other kinds of nonfiction, but they can help young readers get an overall sense of a particular time and place or a person and their important achievements.

Here are six recently published examples:

> *Joan Proctor, Dragon Doctor: The Woman Who Loved Reptiles* by Patricia Valdez
>
> *Karl's New Beak* by Lela Nargi
>
> *Planting Stories: The Life of Librarian and Storyteller Pura Belpré* by Anika Aldamuy Denise
>
> *Spooked! How a Radio Broadcast and* The War of the Worlds *Sparked the 1938 Invasion of America* by Gail Jarrow
>
> *Two Brothers, Four Hands: The Artists Alberto and Diego Giacometti* by Jan Greenberg and Sandra Jordan
>
> *You're Invited to a Moth Ball: A Nighttime Insect Celebration* by Loree Griffin Burns

Typical Features of Narrative Nonfiction

- Narrative writing style
- Tells a story or conveys an experience
- Real characters, scenes, dialogue, narrative arc
- Strong voice and rich, engaging language
- Chronological sequence structure
- Books about people (biographies), events, or processes

Expository Literature

As we mentioned in Chapter 1, after the U.S. Congress passed the No Child Left Behind Act of 2001, school funding priorities suddenly shifted. School library budgets were slashed, and many school librarians lost their jobs. Around the same time, a national economic recession threatened public library budgets too.

By the mid-2000s, the proliferation of websites made straightforward, kid-friendly information widely available without cost, which meant traditional survey books about lions or earthquakes or the Boston Tea Party were no longer mandatory purchases for libraries.

TEACHING **TIP**

Please note that although "expository literature" is the only 5 Kinds of Nonfiction category name that includes the word *expository*, traditional nonfiction, browseable nonfiction, and active nonfiction (discussed on pages 19–20) also have an expository writing style. Only narrative nonfiction has a narrative writing style.

As nonfiction book sales to schools and libraries slumped, authors, illustrators, and publishers began searching for new ways to add value to their work, so they could compete with the Internet. The result has been a new breed of finely crafted expository literature that delights as well as informs.

What exactly is expository literature? According to the *Oxford English Dictionary* (ND), *literature* is defined as "written works, especially those considered of superior or lasting artistic merit," and so *expository literature* can be thought of as writing that explains, describes, or informs with superior or lasting artistic merit (Stewart and Young 2018). The artistry in these books is the result of such characteristics as innovative format, carefully chosen text structure, strong voice, and rich, engaging language.

Unlike traditional nonfiction, expository literature often presents narrowly focused topics or specialized ideas, such as STEM (Science, Technology, Engineering, and Math) concepts, in creative ways that reflect the author's passion for the subject. For example, in the traditional nonfiction book *Butterflies* by Seymour Simon, children learn all about the graceful insects. The book has a standard format in which each double-page spread features one page of text and one full-page photo. The author employs a Description text structure and uses concise, straightforward language.

But the expository literature title *A Butterfly Is Patient* by Dianna Hutts Aston focuses on a butterfly's most amazing characteristics. The book has an innovative format

with two layers of text, stunning art, and a dynamic design. The author presents the information with a wondrous, lyrical voice and makes expert use of such language devices as imagery and personification, inviting readers to think about and appreciate butterflies in a whole new way.

Because expository literature titles are so carefully crafted, they work especially well as mentor texts in writing workshop (Stewart and Young 2019). They can also help students recognize patterns, think by analogy, and engage in big picture thinking.

Here are six recently published examples:

Homes in the Wild: Where Baby Animals and Their Parents Live by Lita Judge

The Next President: The Unexpected Beginnings and Unwritten Future of America's Presidents by Kate Messner

Rotten: Vultures, Beetles, Slime, and Nature's Other Decomposers by Anita Sanchez

We Are Grateful: Otsaliheliga by Traci Sorell

What If You Had T. rex *Teeth? And Other Dinosaur Parts* by Sandra Markle

Women in Art: 50 Fearless Creatives Who Inspired the World by Rachel Ignotofsky

Active Nonfiction

Active nonfiction has been around since at least the 1980s, but thanks to the maker movement, these books have really hit their stride in recent years (Rosen 2017). Active nonfiction titles are highly interactive and/or teach skills that readers can use to engage in an activity. Written with an expository writing style, these field guides, craft books, cookbooks, books of scientific experiments, book-model combinations, and so on are richly designed and carefully formatted to make the information and procedures they present clear and accessible.

These books, which are currently extremely popular with young readers, are the perfect addition to school and library makerspaces.

Here are six recently published examples:

National Geographic Kids Bird Guide of North America by Jonathan Alderfer

Code This! Puzzles, Games, Challenges, and Computer Coding Concepts for the Problem Solver in You by Jennifer Szymanski

Typical Features of Active Nonfiction

- Highly interactive and/or teaches skills for engaging in an activity
- How-to guides, field guides, cookbooks, craft books
- Clear, straightforward language
- Expository writing style

Cooking Class Global Feast! 44 Recipes That Celebrate the World's Cultures by Deanna F. Cook

Hair-Raising Hairstyles That Make a Statement by Rebecca Rissman

Ralph Masiello's Alien Drawing Book by Ralph Masiello

Wildlife Ranger Action Guide: Track, Spot & Provide Healthy Habitat for Creatures Close to Home by Mary Kay Carson

What's in a Name?

Melissa first came across the term "active nonfiction" in 2017 while reading an article in *Publishers Weekly*. It was used by Kristen McLean, director of new business development at Nielsen Book/Nielsen Entertainment, while reporting on Nielsen BookScan data at the American Booksellers Association's Annual Children's Institute Conference. Melissa knew this category would make a perfect addition to her nonfiction classification system.

Looking Ahead

In biology, classification helps us (1) make sense of the diversity of life, (2) understand how living things are related to one another, and (3) communicate our thoughts and ideas about living things more effectively. Classifying nonfiction into five major categories has similar benefits.

As we mentioned earlier in this chapter and will discuss in greater detail in Chapter 4, sorting nonfiction children's books based on key characteristics of the writing and presentation helps readers understand how to access information quickly and easily as well as which titles are best suited for a wide range of uses, including as resources for

Seventh graders sorting books using the 5 Kinds of Nonfiction classification system

conducting research and as mentor texts for informational writing.

Once you understand how classifying books can help students as they read and write nonfiction, we delve deeply into some key elements of nonfiction: text patterns (Chapter 5), text structures (Chapter 6), and voice, language, and point of view (Chapter 7).

Chapter 8 offers innovative and engaging ideas for sharing a diverse array of nonfiction with students. To conclude the book, Chapter 9 introduces the term "blended nonfiction" (books that include characteristics of two or more of the five categories) and explains how these titles can serve as "gateway nonfiction" (books that help students transition from the nonfiction they read with enthusiasm in elementary school to the more rigorous, long-form nonfiction they must read in middle school and high school). The chapter then provides ideas for helping all children interact successfully with both nonfiction writing styles—narrative and expository—as well as all 5 Kinds of Nonfiction.

But before exploring any of these topics, it's critically important to flesh out some of the ideas we briefly mentioned in our author notes at the beginning of this book. That's why Chapter 3 presents academic research suggesting that the way you and your students think about nonfiction may be quite different. And understanding that difference can help you improve the effectiveness of your instruction. So turn the page and dig in!

CHAPTER **3**

Why Students Need Access to a Diverse Array of Nonfiction

"It's inevitable that a reader poring over a compelling nonfiction book is soon swarmed by peers eager for a look themselves."

—Stephanie Harvey and Annie Ward, *From Striving to Thriving: How to Grow Confident, Capable Readers*

What Kind of Books Do You Prefer?

Let's start this chapter with a quick activity.

1. Make a list of five children's books you love.

2. Put a check mark next to the ones that are nonfiction. If none of them are nonfiction, don't worry. You aren't alone.

3. Okay, let's try again. Make a list of five nonfiction children's books you admire.

4. Place an *N* next to the books with a narrative writing style. As we discussed in Chapter 1, these books tell a true story or convey and experience.

5. Place an *E* next to the books with an expository writing style. As we discussed in Chapter 1, these titles inform, describe, or explain.

6. Look at your list. Do you seem to prefer one writing style over the other? If so, why do you think you have that preference?

What Kind of Books Do Most Educators Prefer?

While it's important to understand your own nonfiction writing style preferences, it's also important to understand the preferences of your colleagues and of educators in general. Are you reinforcing one another's thinking? Do you have different ideas and attitudes that you aren't even aware of?

To find out, try the following activity at an upcoming faculty meeting or professional development workshop.

Before other teachers arrive, write the word NARRATIVE on a piece of paper, and tape it to the wall on the right-hand side of the room. Write the word EXPOSITORY on a second piece of paper, and tape it to the wall on the left-hand side of the room. Write the word BOTH on a third piece of paper, and tape it to the wall at the back of the room.

When everyone is ready to begin, briefly discuss the difference between narrative nonfiction and expository nonfiction. Then read aloud the two exemplar books you were introduced to in Chapter 1, *Red-Eyed Tree Frog* (narrative) and *Frog or Toad? How Do You Know?* (expository). Interacting with these books should give everyone a clear understanding of the two writing styles.

Invite participants who prefer fiction and narrative nonfiction to stand near the NARRATIVE sign. Ask colleagues who prefer texts with an expository writing style to stand near the EXPOSITORY sign, and encourage attendees who enjoy both writing styles equally to stand near the BOTH sign.

What do you predict will be the results of this activity? Which of the three groups do you think will be the largest?

In 2018, Melissa conducted this activity with more than 1,000 educators who participated in K–5 professional development workshops or attended literacy or school librarian conferences. Here are the results:

As you look at the tables on page 25, you will notice that the data offer additional evidence of a strong preference for narratives among literacy leaders. Since 2001, when the Robert F. Sibert Informational Book Medal was first awarded, the teacher-librarians, public librarians, and literacy educators who served as judges for the American Library Association's highly respected Youth Media Awards have chosen narrative nonfiction titles again and again.

As Table 3.1 shows, 97 percent of the nonfiction award *winners* had a narrative writing style. In nineteen years, only one expository nonfiction book was selected, and that book was honored for its *art*, not its writing.

TABLE 3.1 American Library Association Youth Media Award Winners, 2001-2019

Writing Style	Printz Award	Newbery Medal	Caldecott Medal	YALSA* Award	Sibert Medal	Total
Narrative	1	0	3	10	19	33
Expository	0	0	1	0	0	1
Blended	0	0	0	0	0	0

*The YALSA Excellence in Nonfiction Award was created in 2010.

As Table 3.2 shows, 90 percent of the nonfiction *honor recipients* had a narrative writing style. About 6 percent of the honor titles had an expository writing style, and about 4 percent had a roughly equal blend of narrative and expository writing.

TABLE 3.2 American Library Association Youth Media Award Honor Titles, 2001–2019

Writing Style	Printz Award	Newbery Medal	Caldecott Medal	YALSA* Award	Sibert Medal	Total
Narrative	5	8	13	34	51	111
Expository	0	0	1	1	5	7
Blended	0	0	1	2	5	8

*The YALSA Excellence in Nonfiction Award was created in 2010.

Right now, many educators reading this book are nodding their heads. Are you? Do these results match your personal beliefs about reading and literature?

Most people whose jobs involve reading, recommending, and sharing children's literature—book reviewers, awards committee members, school librarians, educators responsible for ELA instruction—value and connect strongly with stories and storytelling. They enjoy reading a wide range of fiction as well as narrative nonfiction, such as the many excellent picture book biographies being published today. They believe that narrative nonfiction receives more starred reviews, garners more awards, and, therefore, ends up on more classroom and library bookshelves than expository nonfiction for one simple reason—it's better.

Because this way of thinking represents an undeniable truth for many educators, it's natural to assume that young readers feel the same way, especially when we hear statements like "humans are hardwired to love story."

One of our goals in writing *5 Kinds of Nonfiction* is to disrupt this way of thinking.

For years, we've both questioned the idea that everyone loves stories. Based on our own experiences as readers and conversations with children and educators, what we've observed is that *some* children are, indeed, naturally drawn to narratives. But other children are more analytical thinkers. They're excited by ideas and information and would rather read expository nonfiction.

These observations are in line with Louise Rosenblatt's Transactional Theory of Reading, which recognizes two different stances (or approaches) to reading—aesthetic and efferent. The difference between the two approaches lies in where the reader's attention is while reading. If readers adopt an aesthetic stance, they're reading for enjoyment and are focused on what's happening to them as they experience the book. In the efferent stance, readers are primarily focused on learning and retaining information

(Rosenblatt 1978). In most cases, students who enjoy fiction and narrative nonfiction are reading with an aesthetic stance. But students who are naturally drawn to facts, figures, ideas, and information tend to approach texts from an efferent stance. As a result, they prefer expository nonfiction.

Based on her experiences with young analytical thinkers, Melissa became concerned that the reading preferences of these students—the scientists, engineers, mathematicians, accountants, computer programmers, electricians, and plumbers of the future—were being undervalued, or even ignored, by educators.

By the spring of 2016, Melissa felt so strongly about this issue that she decided to take a sabbatical from writing and conduct a study of elementary students' reading preferences. Because she had no idea how to structure or conduct this kind of study, she dove into the academic literature. And that's when her mind was blown.

The research already existed, and it was powerful. Why, she wondered, didn't more people know about it?

One of the articles Melissa discovered was Marlene's action research study of kindergartners' reading preferences described in Marlene's author note at the beginning of this book. We've been discussing nonfiction and its use in the classroom ever since, and *5 Kinds of Nonfiction* is an outgrowth of our conversations.

What Kind of Books Do Children Prefer?

One of the research studies that we'd like more educators to know about was published in 2017 by Repaskey, Schumm, and Johnson. It reveals the reading preferences of elementary students:

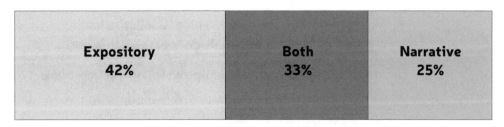

| Expository 42% | Both 33% | Narrative 25% |

When we share this visual in professional development workshops, there's often an audible gasp. This study—and others like it—expose a systemic bias we must work to recognize and address.

A growing body of research offers clear evidence that many students think differently than the adults who are teaching them (Correia 2011; Doiron 2003; Maloch and Horsey 2013; Mohr 2006; Pappas 1991). Rather than craving an emotional connection with the central figure in a book, these children read with a purpose—to understand the world and how it works and their place in it. They want to understand the past and the present, so they can envision the future stretching out before them.

> "Nonfiction is better than fiction because it has real, helpful facts about life."
>
> —Kelsey, fourth grader

These students are captivated by fact-filled books, and they're most likely to develop a love of reading if they have access to expository nonfiction with clear main ideas and supporting details, intriguing patterns, statistics, analogies, concepts, and calculations.

What Kind of Books Do Your Students Prefer?

Are you curious about your own students' preferences for narrative versus expository texts? To find out which writing style your students prefer, try interviewing them during a reading conference. You can ask K–2 students the following questions:

- Do you prefer to read fiction or nonfiction? Why?

- I notice in your browsing box that you've selected a lot of _____. Are these the books you enjoy reading? What is it about them that you like?

- What kinds of books do you enjoy reading at home? What other kinds of materials do you read at home?

You can ask students in grade 3 and up the following questions:

- Do you prefer to read fiction, narrative nonfiction, or expository nonfiction? Why?

- I notice that you often bring back a lot of _____ from the school library. Are these the books you enjoy reading? What is it about them that you like?

- What kinds of books do you enjoy reading at home? What other kinds of materials do you read at home?

You can also make important discoveries about your students' reading preferences by talking to them about the books they choose to look at or bring in from home.

For a more objective and systematic look at your students' reading preferences, you can collect data about the books they choose to read during a specified time frame, such as a week or a month. If your class visits the school library on a regular basis, ask the librarian to use the

A first grader explains why she loves this expository nonfiction book.

school's digital library management system, such as the Follett Destiny® Library Manager™, to track the titles the children check out. Then work with the librarian to sort the titles into three categories—fiction, narrative nonfiction, and expository nonfiction. The results may surprise you.

When Marlene reviewed library data for one of the elementary schools she works with, she discovered that kindergarten and first-grade students were checking out very few nonfiction titles. It turns out the librarian preselected books the students could check out and placed them on a table. Unfortunately, the librarian was making only fiction titles available to students. Like many educators, she mistakenly believed that students prefer fiction.

At a middle school, Marlene found that grade 6 students were checking out fewer nonfiction titles than she expected. It turns out that most of the books were being used for a book talk assignment, and the list of suggested titles included no nonfiction. Once teachers let their classes know that they could choose a nonfiction title for their book talk, students began checking out more nonfiction.

When teacher-librarian Ray Doiron monitored student book preferences at his elementary school on Prince Edward Island, he initially found that students checked out twice as much nonfiction as fiction. Both he and the teachers were astonished.

After interviewing the children, Doiron realized that some of the nonfiction books were being used for classroom assignments. To gain a stronger sense of the students' actual reading preferences, Doiron repeated the process, focusing on just the books students were *choosing* to read. Over three years, he collected data for 10,000 library transactions among students in grades 1–6 and found that a whopping 40 percent of the checkouts were nonfiction titles the students were reading for pleasure (Doiron 2003).* These results showcase just how much some students really do prefer nonfiction. Do you think the results would be similar for your students?

While Doiron's results are illuminating, you can learn plenty of valuable information with a much shorter study that involves just the students in your classroom (Bukowiecki and Correia 2017). Using your own observations from conferring with readers as well as the data you and your school's librarian collect together, you can (1) evaluate the choices of individual students to look for patterns and (2) analyze the entire classroom data set to answer the following questions:

- How many children checked out expository texts each week?

- Did students show any preferences for a particular kind of nonfiction—active, browseable, traditional, expository literature, narrative?

- What topics are "hot" among your students right now?

- Does your classroom book collection match the interests of your students?

---

*Although Doiron did not differentiate narrative nonfiction and expository nonfiction, it is likely that most, if not all, of the nonfiction had an expository writing style because very little narrative nonfiction was being published for children at the time the study was conducted.

- Do the books you select for instruction match the interests of your students?

- Are your striving readers choosing expository nonfiction? If so, do they seem to prefer a particular topic? Do they seem to have a category preference—active, browseable, traditional, or expository literature?

This last bullet point is critically important because, although some info-loving kids manage to develop as readers despite having little exposure to expository books, others don't. Instead, they receive the unfortunate label "reluctant reader." Research shows that expository nonfiction motivates these students, and they're significantly more likely to thrive as readers if they have access to expository nonfiction on topics of personal interest. In other words, for them, expository nonfiction is the gateway to literacy (Cambria and Guthrie 2010; Dreher and Kletzien 2015; Jobe and Dayton-Sakari 2002; Moss and Hendershot 2002).

But that's not the only reason to fill classrooms and libraries with a diverse array of finely crafted expository books. Routinely using high-quality expository nonfiction as part of instruction benefits fact-loving kids AND their classmates too.

Expository Nonfiction in the Classroom

Take a moment to think about your instruction. Do you tend to focus your reading and writing lessons around fiction? When you select non-fiction to support the content-area curriculum, do you usually choose books with a narrative writing style? If you find yourself favoring fiction and narrative nonfiction, you aren't alone. But to honor the reading preferences of all students, it's important to include expository titles, too. In this section, we discuss some of the ways integrating the four kinds of expository nonfiction—active nonfiction, browseable nonfiction, traditional nonfiction, and expository literature—into your ELA and content-area lessons can improve the literacy skills of your entire class.

Building Content Knowledge

Think about that student in your class who's fascinated by and seems to know everything about dinosaurs. How did she become a mini-expert? How did she learn their long, complex scientific names and other key vocabulary terms? How does she keep track of when and where they lived, what they ate, and all their unique body features? In other words, how did that child build her content knowledge?

Chances are it wasn't by reading a textbook cover to cover. The child most likely built knowledge over time by interacting with the information in a variety of ways—viewing dinosaur videos, studying and drawing pictures of dinosaurs, talking incessantly about dinosaurs to anyone who would listen, and, undoubtedly, by reading dozens of expository nonfiction children's books about dinosaurs.

Not all students are interested in dinosaurs, but every child is curious about something.

Rockets

Rain forests

Pets

Pirates

Bicycles

Ballet

Discovering a student's passion and fueling it with high-quality nonfiction can make all the difference in their progress as a reader. These books can inspire students to stretch their knowledge and understanding of the world around them.

Today's students crave experiences that go beyond where they are or what they can access. Reading expository nonfiction can help them feel connected to distant places without having to leave home. For example, many students are fascinated by what life is like for children their own age in other countries. They're excited to learn how animals survive in the freezing-cold Arctic and the sizzling-hot desert. With today's technology, we can pair high-quality nonfiction books with webcams, videos, and social media tools to transport our students virtually anywhere.

Study after study shows that finely crafted children's books with an expository writing style can enrich content-area learning by motivating and engaging a broad range of students (Beers and Probst 2016; Duke, Bennett-Armistead, and Roberts 2003; Hirsch and Hansel 2013). They feature rich, precise language; stunning visuals; and dynamic format and design that introduce and reinforce ideas and information in a clear, lively, age-appropriate way.

By delighting as well as informing, these books cultivate the development of critical literacy skills, such as fluency and comprehension. Because expository nonfiction is often jam-packed with detailed information, engaged readers willingly choose to read the text (or portions of the text) multiple times. They're also excited to read the text aloud to anyone who will listen, so they can share what they've discovered. This kind of repeated, deep reading builds fluency (Rasinksi 2014).

As motivated readers navigate high-interest expository text, they often pause to ponder and digest the content that's new to them. They may also sketch pictures to help them remember chunks of information. Educators teach these strategies to all readers, regardless of genre, but when students are truly engaged by the text and have a deep desire to learn, they're more likely to apply the strategies independently.

High-quality children's nonfiction books can also help students learn the technical and specialized vocabulary that Beck, McKeown, and Kucan (2013) refer to as "tier 3 words" in an authentic and inviting context. In these carefully designed, visually engaging titles, vocabulary is often supported by photographs, diagrams, charts, infographics, and other text features that help students derive the meaning of new words. These visuals are especially helpful for English language learners who require extra instructional scaffolding when learning content and vocabulary. For all students, discovering new words while reading about high-interest topics is fun and effective, and the rich, precise language may even work its way into the students' writing. Let's face it . . . learning vocabulary in this engaging, authentic way sure beats receiving a list of words and looking up definitions!

Understanding Complex Texts

When elementary readers have access to plenty of expository nonfiction, they have lots of opportunities to discover and explore the key elements of this writing style and develop the ability to read increasingly complex writing as they move from one grade level to the next (Beers and Probst 2016). As a result, these books prepare students for later encounters with textbooks and other educational materials with terse, rigorous expository text.

Because reading aloud is such a powerful teaching tool, we devote an entire section to this educational strategy in Chapter 8. But at this point, we'd like to briefly discuss using it to model how students can comprehend challenging expository texts as they read independently. To maximize the benefits of reading aloud, we recommend reading and analyzing books in advance. During this process, ask yourself the following questions:

- Do my students have the background knowledge needed to understand this book? If not, how can I prepare them?

- Which comprehension strategies can I demonstrate while reading this book?

- What vocabulary knowledge do students need to comprehend this complex text? What is the most effective way to share these unfamiliar words?

Knowing a book's specific comprehension challenges before reading it to students will allow you to provide the instructional scaffolding your class needs to understand and appreciate the text.

As you read a book aloud, we recommend modeling questions students can ask themselves as they attempt to access and understand the content. Examples include:

- Does this book match my purpose for reading?

- How do I monitor what I'm reading to make sure I understand the information?

- What do I do when I come to a part I don't understand?

- What if I'm reading for a particular purpose? Do I need to read cover to cover?

- How do I know where to find what I need?

The more experience children have interacting with expository nonfiction, the more capable they'll become in asking and answering these kinds of questions.

Evaluating Complex Texts

When educators model what Beers and Probst refer to as "reading with a skeptical eye," students will realize the importance of (1) evaluating the ideas and information in a book for accuracy and (2) determining whether the author's conclusions are logical, reasonable, and inclusive. As students read with this purpose in mind, they should ask the following questions:

- Is the information accurate and up-to-date?

- Is the author biased?

- Does the author present a variety of perspectives? Whose perspective is highlighted/ignored?

- Does the author omit an important set of facts, voice, or point of view?

Teachers and librarians can help students practice thinking about expository text this way by sharing books like *Boy, Were We Wrong About Dinosaurs!* by Kathleen Kudlinski, which emphasizes the importance of evaluating ideas and thinking critically by highlighting mistakes that scientists made in the past and how our thinking evolves over time.

You could also read aloud excerpts from two books or articles with contradictory facts or statistics about the same topic. When you are done reading, divide the class into small groups and encourage the teams to investigate the discrepancy. Is one book out of date? What are the authors' sources? Which set of sources seems more reliable and authoritative? Is one author relying too heavily on a particular source? When students have experience scrutinizing text in this way, they learn the value of looking at everything they read through a critical lens rather than just accepting what's written as fact.

Writing to Communicate Information

Because writing expository text is a critically important way of summarizing, synthesizing, and communicating thoughts and ideas, it's the style of nonfiction writing students will be required to produce most frequently throughout their school years and in their future jobs (Stead and Hoyt 2012).

Whether they're writing a report, a thesis, a business proposal, or a company newsletter, college students and workers need to craft expository prose that's clear, logical, and interesting. The sooner and more often children have opportunities to read and write expository nonfiction, the better off they'll be in school and in life. As we'll discuss in detail in Chapter 4, children's books with an expository writing style make ideal mentor texts for modeling these critical skills.

A senior elementary education major writing a final research paper

Preparing Students for Standardized Tests

Like it or not, state-mandated testing is probably here to stay—at least for a while—so it's important to understand how access to expository nonfiction can help students meet the challenges of that testing (Duke 2014; Moss 2008; Pilonieta 2011; Shanahan 2012).

Currently, ELA standards call for a large proportion of students' reading and writing to be informational text, and standardized tests reflect this heightened focus. The Progress in International Reading Literacy Study (PIRLS) is a standardized test given to a select number of fourth graders throughout the world every five years. The PIRLS framework stipulates that half of the passages should assess "reading for literary experience" and half should assess "reading to acquire and use information" (Mullis, Martin, Foy, and Drucker 2012).

We see this same trend in U.S. state testing. Students are routinely required to read complex expository passages and answer related questions. In some cases, students are expected to analyze and synthesize information from multiple texts before writing a response. The more exposure, modeling, and practice students have with reading, writing, listening, and studying expository nonfiction, the better prepared they'll be to apply the skills they've learned in testing situations.

Rethinking Your Book Collection

By now, you're probably wondering how you can make sure that your students have access to a diverse array of nonfiction texts. With that goal in mind, we encourage you to take a moment to evaluate your own classroom or library book collection.

- Do you have enough nonfiction titles? Experts recommend a fifty-fifty mix of fiction and nonfiction (Dreher and Kletzein 2015), with at least two-thirds of the nonfiction having an expository writing style.

- How diverse is your nonfiction section? Does it include a healthy selection of books from all five categories—active, browseable, traditional, expository literature, and narrative?

Sadly, studies show that, in U.S. classrooms, only 17 to 22 percent of all titles available to students for independent reading are nonfiction and only 7 to 9 percent have an expository writing style (Dreher and Kletzein 2015). In other words, fewer than 10 percent of the books in a typical classroom collection feature four out of the five categories of books in the 5 Kinds of Nonfiction classification system. This is a statistic that needs to change!

Although similar data isn't available for school libraries, as you may recall from Chapter 2, according to a 2016 report from the National Education Association, only 61.9 percent of elementary schools have a full-time state-certified librarian/media specialist (Tuck and Holmes 2016). As a result, it's likely that many school libraries do not have a well-balanced, up-to-date nonfiction collection.

Because we want all children to become enthusiastic readers and develop a love of language, it's critically important to give students access to a broad assortment of high-quality fiction, narrative nonfiction, and expository nonfiction titles. To rebalance your collection in a way that makes sense in terms of student reading preferences and how the books can best be used in a school setting, we'd like to suggest striving for the percentages shown in Table 3.3.

TABLE 3.3 How to Rebalance Your Book Collection

Category	Pleasure Reading	Research	Mentor Text	Percentage
Narrative	X		X	20%
Expository Literature	X	X	X	25%
Traditional	X	X		20%
Browseable	X	X	X	25%
Active*	X			10%

*This table assumes that your school has a designated makerspace with plenty of active nonfiction. If this is not the case, aim to add a bit more active nonfiction to your school's classroom and library collections.

Throughout the rest of the book, we'll discuss the rationale behind our recommended percentages and describe how books in each category can and should be used to engage fact-loving kids and to enrich instruction.

CHAPTER 4

How Understanding the 5 Kinds of Nonfiction Helps Readers and Writers

"Nonfiction should be read for enjoyment, learning, and wonder! It helps readers learn truths that form the basis of real life. The 5 Kinds of Nonfiction classification system enables students to view nonfiction through new lenses, affording them the opportunity to think more deeply and critically about the format and presentation of content."

—Ruth McKoy Lowery, professor of literacy, University of North Texas, Denton, Texas

Teaching the 5 Kinds of Nonfiction to Students

Before students can reap the benefits of the 5 Kinds of Nonfiction classification system, they need to learn the characteristics of each category and have practical experience sorting and interacting with a wide variety of nonfiction books. The following activities are a great way to get started.

ACTIVITY 4.1

Introducing the 5 Kinds of Nonfiction Children's Books

TEACHING **TIP**

Please feel free to adapt the activities in this book to meet the specific needs of your students, schedule, and classroom setup. Many of the activities can be folded into minilessons or presented as stand-alone activities. Some can be completed in one class period, while others may require several days.

Organize students into small groups and invite each team to gather a variety of nonfiction books on a single broad topic from the school library. Possibilities include outer space, ancient civilizations, or natural disasters. After the children have sorted the books into at least three categories that make sense to them, compare the criteria each team used. Be sure to let the class know that each group's set of criteria is valid and well thought out.

Next, introduce the 5 Kinds of Nonfiction classification system. After sharing several books that fit each category, read aloud sections of

"Giving students the opportunity to go through the books first without direct instruction really pushed them to engage with the texts and played on their natural curiosity to organize and make sense of the seemingly random materials."
—Abi Diaz, language arts/social studies teacher, Carl Sandburg
　　Middle School, Mundelein, Illinois

books that are about the same topic but represent different book types. The following is one possible text set:

- *National Geographic Kids Bird Guide of North America* by Jonathan Alderfer (active)
- *Eyewitness Books: Bird* by David Burnie (browseable)
- *Penguins* by Seymour Simon (traditional)
- *Feathers: Not Just for Flying* by Melissa Stewart (expository literature)
- *City Hawk: The Story of Pale Male* by Megan McCarthy (narrative)

> *"What seemed to be most helpful for students was looking at five texts around the same topic and noticing the nuances of each type. . . . [W]e had rich and engaging discussions, and what some may call 'debates,' as we tried to categorize each book."*
>
> —Kristen Picone, fifth-grade teacher, RJO Intermediate School, Kings Park, New York

The sample books listed in Chapter 2 can guide you in identifying other suitable titles in your own school library or classroom collection.

Ask students to compare how the books present information. Is the focus broad, or is a specific concept being discussed? What kind of text features does each book include? What kind of text structure, writing style, and craft moves does the author employ? Does the writing have a distinct voice? What similarities and differences do students notice across the categories?

Finally, give each team a copy of the Category Feature Cards in Appendix D. After students take a few minutes to review the information, send the groups back to the stacks to gather a selection of nonfiction books on a new topic. (Asking

Third graders sorting books using the 5 Kinds of Nonfiction classification system

students to gather a new set of books rather than resort their original pile reinforces the idea that there are many ways to sort books and that there was nothing "wrong" with their initial classification.)

Invite each team to sort the books into the five types—active, browseable, traditional, expository literature, and narrative. Did they find examples of all five kinds? If not, can they explain why? (For example, some topics may not lend themselves to active titles or a narrative approach.)

ACTIVITY 4.2

Reinforcing the 5 Kinds of Nonfiction Children's Books

Remind students of the 5 Kinds of Nonfiction by sharing a few exemplar books from each category. Then divide the class into small groups and encourage the teams to brainstorm a few characteristics of each type—active, browseable, traditional, expository literature, and narrative. If students struggle with this task, you may wish to give each team a copy of the Category Feature Cards in Appendix D.

Next, give each group a packet of sticky notes and three to six books from various categories. Encourage students to classify the books and label each one with a sticky note. When all the teams have completed this task, ask each group to rotate to a different station, leaving their books behind. Students should review the books at their new station and discuss how the previous group classified each title. If they disagree with the previous group, they should add a second sticky note explaining their rationale.

Repeat this process until each group has reviewed all the books. Then have a brief class discussion about books that have multiple sticky notes on them. Finally, ask the class to brainstorm ways that knowing these categories can help them as readers and writers.

When Marlene did these activities with a class of eighth-grade students at a suburban school in Massachusetts, she discovered that the students had never thought about ways to categorize nonfiction. As students sorted the books, they skimmed through the pages and read short excerpts. They compared books to one another, and, in some cases, debated about how a particular book should be classified. Marlene was impressed by how the students used the criteria listed on the Category Feature Cards as rationale for their thinking. Overall, the students seemed most familiar with traditional nonfiction and could most easily recognize active nonfiction.

During the second activity, when the teams rotated to new stations, the students generally agreed with their peers' decisions about how the books should be classified. But as their discussions continued, one group noticed that some books could be classified in more than one way. In other words, they "discovered" blended nonfiction (books that include characteristics of two or more categories), which we discuss in detail in Chapter 9.

After completing these activities, the students evaluated the experience of classifying nonfiction and explained how they thought knowing the 5 Kinds of Nonfiction could help them as learners. Here are two students' comments.

> *"I think it would be very helpful to categorize nonfiction into five types because it allows you to get a better understanding of the book's purpose and the ways the book can best be used to suit your needs and interests."* —Eoin, eighth grader

> *"Today's activity showed me that one topic can be written [about] in many different types of nonfiction books. So, it would be helpful to find a book about weather projects without going through books with just facts about weather."* —Jocelyn, eighth grader

We also asked Valerie Bang-Jensen, a professor of education at a small college in Vermont, to try these activities with some of her undergraduate and graduate students and record their thinking. We were curious to see how their comments would be similar to and different from those of the younger students. Here are some of the samples.

> *"Just knowing there are different types of nonfiction has led me to look at all nonfiction through a different lens. Different kinds may cater to different audiences."* —Matt, graduate student

> *"This classification system . . . emphasizes the importance of teaching all types of nonfiction, each for its own purpose. Five is an easy number to work with, and each type of text stands out compared to the rest."* —Aubrey, graduate student

> *"The five classifications can help students target texts appropriate for various stages of research."* —Morgan, graduate student

> *"These categories may be applied to nearly any nonfiction book. The system can help readers learn about their preferences within nonfiction."* —Shannon, undergraduate student

> *"The clear examples can help teachers choose mentor texts. It can also inspire students to think of their audience and the purpose of their writing."* —Maria, graduate student

Applying the 5 Kinds of Nonfiction

As we briefly mentioned in Chapter 2, once students understand the 5 Kinds of Nonfiction and have experience classifying books according to this system, they'll be able to predict (1) the type of information they're likely to find in a book and (2) how that information will be presented.

For example, consider two books about Benjamin Franklin. A quick preview of *Benjamin Franklin, American Genius: His Life and Ideas with 21 Activities* by Brandon Marie Miller makes it clear that this book is active nonfiction.

It includes a thorough biographical account of Franklin's life presented with a Chronological Sequence text structure, plenty of black-and-white photos, and activities that highlight his important ideas and inventions.

Now & Ben: The Modern Inventions of Benjamin Franklin by Gene Barretta is quite different. Although there is some overlapping content, Barretta's title is chockful of colorful, humorous illustrations and features a compelling Compare & Contrast text structure that highlights how we make use of Franklin's many ideas and inventions in the modern world.

Even though both books focus on the same man, because one is active nonfiction and the other is expository literature, they have different kinds of information and different ways of presenting the material. A student who is familiar with the 5 Kinds of Nonfiction can quickly evaluate the books, identify their differences, and determine which one is better suited for their purpose. The student can also decide which book they are more likely to enjoy reading.

Discovering a Favorite Kind of Nonfiction

Research shows that lifelong readers have strong reading preferences and can easily self-select books that meet their needs and interests (Miller and Kelley 2014). But no one is born with this skill. It grows over time as readers repeatedly make choices on their own and learn from their mistakes. If we want today's students to develop a deep and lasting love of reading, we must give them similar opportunities. Only then can they learn to value themselves as readers and as decisions makers (Miller and Sharp 2018).

Why is choosing a book so powerful for students? It gives them a sense of ownership over their reading lives, which increases their motivation and their comprehension (Guthrie et al. 2007). When students are personally invested, they're more likely to stay engaged as they struggle to understand challenging passages.

When it comes to reading for pleasure, you may not turn to nonfiction, but, as we discussed in Chapter 3, many of your students will—if they're given the chance. As students select nonfiction for independent reading, topic will undoubtedly be a key factor, but when students can predict the type of information in a book and how that information is presented, they can make more informed decisions.

For example, imagine a student who suddenly develops an interest in the weather and wants to start reading about it. If that child has experience using the 5 Kinds of Nonfiction classification system, they will know that traditional nonfiction books and browseable nonfiction books can both provide the broad, general introduction the student is looking for. The child will also know that, in all likelihood, both types of books will have a Description text structure and an expository writing style.

If the student is a skilled reader who's interested in a straightforward, systematic presentation, they may select a traditional nonfiction title, such as *Weather* by Seymour Simon. But if the child is a striving reader, they may decide that the short text blocks in a browseable book, such as *Ultimate Weather-pedia* by Stephanie Warren Drimmer, are more appealing. A visual learner might also prefer *Ultimate Weather-pedia* because it features rich art and dynamic design. When students understand the 5 Kinds of Nonfiction, they have a powerful tool for self-selecting books they'll love.

Here are some examples of why students gravitate toward specific kinds of nonfiction books.

I like **active nonfiction** because . . .

"it teaches you to do the things you want to do." —Gina, fourth grader

"you get to do things while you read. That makes me feel calmer." —Jack, fourth grader

"when you close the book, you are left with inspiration and creativity." —Lucy, fifth grader

I like **browseable books** because . . .

"you open it to any page and find a cool fact, and I like reading cool facts because they teach me about stuff." —Lily, second grader

"you have a lot of choices about how you read. It's like the potluck dinners at my church." —Matthew, fourth grader

"I can learn a ton of new, and sometimes crazy, facts. I like to learn new facts so I can share them with family and friends." —Clara, fourth grader

"I like the design. I prefer to flip through the pages to find exactly what I am looking for rather than have to read through a whole book. I especially like illustrations, photos, and captions in nonfiction texts and browseable usually has a lot of them." —Keith, fifth grader

I like **expository literature** because . . .

"it has facts plus it can make you think about something in a new way." —Rowan, fourth grader

"it can surprise you. And sometimes it's like playing a game." —Ryan, fourth grader

"it's a fun way to learn." —Josephine, fourth grader

"it teaches you things that you didn't know you wanted to learn about." —Braelyn, fourth grader

"it's all about an idea with lots of surprising or interesting examples." —Madeline, fifth grader

I like **narrative nonfiction** because . . .

> *"it has characters and a story that is a real situation! It is like I Survived and other fiction books."* —Miles, second grader

> *"it's like a story, and being the fiction lover, I love stories."* —Dwight, fourth grader

> *"I'm not a nonfiction type, so it really helps me learn more without having to read constant facts."* —Flynn, fourth grader

> *"I like reading biographies about real people that include dialogue and other narrative elements."* —Thomas, fifth grader

> *"I love reading, telling, and writing stories. Sometimes when I read a narrative nonfiction book, I have [to] ask myself whether it is fiction or nonfiction because it can be hard to tell. Luckily the back matter will usually help me decide."* —Gabby, fifth grader

And, of course, some students will devour any category of book on a subject they're passionate about. Here's an example.

> *"I like any book from any category as long as it's about sharks. That's my favorite topic."* —Asher, fourth grader

It's so, so, SO important for educators to keep comments like these in mind as they add books to their classroom and library book collections and select titles as read-alouds and for instruction.

Identifying the Best Books for a Specific Purpose

According to ground-breaking literacy researcher Louise M. Rosenblatt, "It is important to differentiate purpose at any point in the learning process. . . . [W]henever you are having students read something, have them be clear about their purpose" (Rosenblatt 1999). Highly regarded literacy educator Cris Tovani agrees. She has observed that having a clear purpose affects everything about the reading experience, including a student's ability to remain focused and interested even when the text is challenging (Tovani 2000).

As Table 4.1 shows, once students have established their reason for reading, they can use their knowledge of the 5 Kinds of Nonfiction to identify the best kind(s) of books for their particular purpose.

TABLE 4.1 Best Nonfiction Book Category by Purpose

Student Purpose	Nonfiction Category
Learn about a broad topic in a systematic way	Traditional nonfiction
Learn about a broad topic in digestible chunks or with an emphasis on visuals	Browseable nonfiction
Share fascinating facts with friends	Browseable nonfiction
Understand a past time and place	Narrative nonfiction
Understand how the personality and experiences of a person contributes to their accomplishments	Narrative nonfiction
Understand the processes scientists use to understand the world and how it works	Narrative nonfiction
Understand a focused idea, such as a STEM concept	Expository literature
Learn a new skill	Active nonfiction
Gather research	Early in the process: Traditional nonfiction Later in the process: Browseable nonfiction, expository literature
Use as a mentor text for writing	Procedural writing: Active nonfiction Personal narratives: Narrative nonfiction Informational writing: Expository literature, browseable nonfiction

The categories for the first eight purposes listed in Table 4.1 should be easy to identify once students are familiar with the category features listed in Chapter 2 (and on the Category Feature Cards in Appendix D), but understanding how the 5 Kinds of Nonfiction can assist students while researching and writing deserves a bit of additional explanation.

How the 5 Kinds of Nonfiction Can Support Research

To professional writers, research is like a treasure hunt—a quest for tantalizing tidbits of knowledge. It's an active, self-driven process that requires deep and critical thinking. As authors seek out unique and fascinating information, they think creatively about sources. They ask themselves

Where can I look?

Who can I ask?

How can I search in a new or unexpected way?

Children's book author Loree Griffin Burns hunting for butterflies at Wachusett Meadow Wildlife Sanctuary in Princeton, Massachusetts. Personal observations are a great source of information.

Unfortunately, most students don't bring that kind of creative spirit to their research process. As a result, research seems downright boring to them. Why are students so disconnected from a process that fills professional writers with excitement? Because in many elementary schools, research involves plucking information off fact sheets or using just a few preapproved websites. There's no inquiry, no exploration, no thrill of discovery.

Even when students are allowed to select their own books, they often get bogged down as they aimlessly slog through page after page of text. That really *is* boring.

But just imagine how their mindset would change if they could examine just a few pages of a book and know whether it's likely to be helpful. And furthermore, what if students had the skills necessary to access the desired information quickly and confidently? That's exactly what can happen when students understand the 5 Kinds of Nonfiction.

As students learn to classify books according to this system, they discover that

- Traditional nonfiction is ideal for the early stages of the research process because these books provide a clear, straightforward, age-appropriate overview of a broad topic, allowing students to "read around" their topic and develop a general understanding.

- Browseable books are better suited for the later stages of the research process because it's easy to locate specific bits of information. In addition, these books often contain fun facts that can enrich student writing.

- Expository literature is better suited for the later stages of the research process because these books contain focused information.

- Narrative nonfiction isn't a good choice for research because it can be difficult to locate pertinent information.

- Active nonfiction isn't as likely as other kinds of nonfiction to have the specific facts students need, but it may be able to help them understand a process or technique.

"Having experience with the 5 Kinds of Nonfiction will help students know what to expect when choosing nonfiction to read. When seeking out books for research, students may be able to make more conscious and appropriate choices based on their topic and purpose."

—Kristen Picone, fifth-grade teacher, RJO Intermediate School, Kings Park, New York

Armed with this knowledge, students can become adept at moving back and forth between different kinds of nonfiction books to locate background information and more focused details.

For example, imagine this scenario: A second grader named Kiyana has seen ladybugs in her yard and is excited to write a report about them. Because she doesn't know much about these little insects, she begins her research process by reading a traditional nonfiction book with information about where ladybugs live, what they eat, important body features, and the ladybug lifecycle.

As Kiyana reads, she notices that all the photos in the book are taken in the summer. She wonders what ladybugs are doing during her birthday month—December. To find out, she needs a book with more focused information.

With the help of the school librarian, Kiyana finds the expository literature title *Wait, Rest, Pause: Dormancy in Nature* by Marcie Flinchum Atkins. The book explains that each fall, ladybugs "fatten up, pile up, stiffen up." During the winter they rest in a huddle and share body warmth. Then in spring, the ladybugs "wiggle awake, feast, flit away."

Kiyana is so inspired by the book's rich language that she decides to write about this period of the ladybug's life. But she remembers her teacher saying how important it is for writers to "use their own words" rather than copy from a book.

As Kiyana tries to think of another word for "flit," she returns to the traditional nonfiction title and finds an amazing photo of a ladybug in flight. But it doesn't help her understand how the ladybug moves through the air.

When Kiyana goes home, she decides to get creative with her research. She catches a ladybug in a glass vial and examines it closely. She sees all the body features she read about in school. When Kiyana releases the ladybug, she tries to observe how it flies, but it moves too fast.

As Kiyana wishes there was a way to watch a ladybug in slow motion, she remembers a time-lapsed video her class saw of a plant growing. After dinner, she asks her dad to help her find a YouTube video of a ladybug flying in slow motion, and they find three! Kiyana's able to see exactly how a ladybug unfolds its delicate inner wings as it takes off and then flaps them at top speed as it whizzes through the air. The next day, she uses her observations to add vibrant descriptive language to her report.

By using a combination of books from different nonfiction categories, students can find inspiration and focus their thinking. Then they can stretch beyond these basic sources and embark on a self-driven quest for information from personal observations, interviews, historical artifacts, and more. This is the kind of research that leads to passionate, distinctive nonfiction writing.

How the 5 Kinds of Nonfiction Can Support Informational Writing

While active nonfiction can and should be used as mentor texts for procedural writing and narrative nonfiction will assist and inspire students as they write personal narratives, in this book, our discussion will be weighted toward informational writing.

Why did we make this choice? Because informational writing is the kind of text students will be required to produce most frequently throughout their school years and in their future jobs. Whether they're writing a report, a thesis, a business proposal, or a company newsletter, they'll need to craft informational prose that's clear, logical, and interesting.

As we discussed in Chapter 1, the terms "informational books" and "informational texts" can be confusing because they have several competing definitions. Luckily, the same is not true for "informational writing." Generally speaking, this term refers to prose with an expository writing style. Students are exposed to informational writing as they read textbooks, encyclopedic databases, some magazine articles, and many newspaper articles. But in this guide, we're focusing on using high-quality children's books as mentor texts for informational writing because so much time and care goes into creating them. Besides being meticulously researched and fully faithful to the facts, these titles feature captivating art, dynamic design, and finely crafted prose.

Expository literature is the best overall choice for modeling informational writing because it features so many of the craft moves espoused by state ELA standards, but in some cases, browseable books can also make good mentor texts. And even though narrative nonfiction features a narrative writing style, these books can work well as models for specific standards-based craft moves. Table 4.2 on the next page provides a summary of general recommendations for teaching key characteristics of informational writing. Many of these craft elements will be discussed in greater detail in Chapters 5, 6, and 7.

TABLE 4.2 The Best Kinds of Nonfiction Books for Teaching Craft Moves in Informational Writing

Craft Move	Best Kind(s) of Book	Reason
Compelling beginnings	Expository literature	Browseable nonfiction may lack a strong hook. Narrative nonfiction starts with a scene, which isn't an element of informational writing.
Satisfying endings	Expository literature, narrative nonfiction	Browseable books may lack a conclusion.
Text features	Expository literature, browseable nonfiction	Narrative nonfiction may include some text features, but they're more numerous and diverse in expository literature and browseable nonfiction.
Innovative format	Expository literature, browseable nonfiction	Narrative nonfiction usually flows from page to page with little formatting.
Carefully chosen text structure	Expository literature	Browseable nonfiction typically has a Description text structure, and narrative nonfiction has a Chronological Sequence text structure. Expository literature is the only category with a wide assortment of text structures.
Strong voice	Expository literature, narrative nonfiction	Browseable nonfiction often lacks a distinct voice, but it's often easy to identify in expository literature and narrative nonfiction.
Rich, engaging language	Expository literature, narrative nonfiction	Browseable nonfiction often lacks rich language because these books explore broad, general topics.
Carefully chosen point of view	Expository literature, narrative nonfiction	Browseable nonfiction generally has third-person narration.

You'll notice that Table 4.2 does not include active nonfiction or traditional nonfiction. As we mentioned earlier, active nonfiction is generally better suited for teaching procedural writing than informational writing. And although traditional nonfiction can play an important role during the research process, these books do not provide the best examples of engaging, finely crafted informational writing. For that, expository literature, which presents specialized topics in creative ways that reflect a writer's zeal for the subject, is a better choice (Dorfman and Cappelli 2009; Kiefer 2010).

This has nothing to do with how talented the writers are and everything to do with the inherent differences of writing a broad overview versus taking a more focused approach. Simply put, writing in a generalized way limits a nonfiction writer's ability to craft rich, engaging text (Portalupi and Fletcher 2001).

When writers take an in-depth look at a specific idea, concept, or question, they can be more playful and innovative. They can select a text format and text structure that reflect their unique approach to the content (Clark, Jones, and Reutzel 2013; Kerper 1998; Williams et al. 2007). They can also experiment with voice and language devices (Moss 2003; Stewart and Young 2018). Because writers of traditional nonfiction must cover a huge amount of information in a limited number of words, they don't have the same kind of opportunities to delight as well as inform.

Since the same is true for young writers, we think it's time for elementary educators to stop asking students to write all-about books. Students are most likely to write engaging, high-quality nonfiction when they choose a topic they're excited about and zoom in on a specific idea, concept, or question that allows them to use the nonfiction craft moves they've learned to the best of their ability.

For example, think back to Kiyana—the girl who's curious about ladybugs. Instead of writing an all-about report about ladybugs, she has decided to focus on the insects' behavior during a specific part of the year. The expository literature title that Kiyana read, *Wait, Rest, Pause: Dormancy in Nature*, serves as a source of information, but its rich language also motivates her to think carefully about word choice, especially her description of how ladybugs fly. The book's Cause & Effect text structure and second-person point of view may also influence the way Kiyana writes her report, or perhaps she'll find other mentor texts that inspire her to organize and present the information she's collected in a different way.

When students take this approach to informational writing, they'll craft a rich, engaging text that reflects their passion for their topic. Let's give our young writers a chance to shine!

A Deeper Dive into Nonfiction Craft

Characters

Setting

Plot

Theme

Dialogue

Voice

Point of View

The critical elements of fiction writing have been recognized and taught in schools for more than 150 years, but the tools and terminology for understanding the craft of nonfiction writing are developing right now, within our lifetimes. It's a great time for nonfiction!

Some nonfiction craft moves, such as voice, language devices, and point of view, overlap with fiction craft terms because they refer to elements that can enrich all writing. But craft elements like text features, text format, and text structure are unique to nonfiction and most relevant to expository nonfiction. In Activity 4.3, we have provided lists of questions that can help students at various grade levels learn to enjoy and evaluate both the content and the craftsmanship within high-quality nonfiction books.

Nonfiction Appreciation and Examination

After reading aloud a nonfiction picture book from either the narrative nonfiction or expository literature category, ask students what they liked most about the book. Record their responses on a piece of chart paper labeled "Appreciation."

For grades K and 1, discuss the following questions with your class:

- What is this book about?
- What did you learn from this book? Can you share some examples?
- What are the new and important words you learned?
- Did the author make you want to learn more about this topic? If yes, how did they do that?

For grades 2 and up, after discussing the four questions above with your students, divide the class into small groups and encourage the teams to think carefully about the range of craft elements the author employed while writing the book. Give each group a list with some of the following questions to guide their discussion:

Grade 2 and up

- How did the author hook readers at the beginning?
- Is there anything about how the author has organized the text that makes it easier to read?

- How do photos, illustrations, diagrams, charts, or maps help you understand the information?
- Does the author include text features? If so, how do they help you?

Grade 3 and up

- Does this book have a narrative or expository writing style? Explain your rationale.
- How does the book's format help you understand the information?
- How would you describe the voice of the writing? Can you spot any words or punctuation choices that helped the author create that voice?
- Does the text's voice seem to match the style of the artwork? Explain your rationale.
- Does the book have a satisfying ending? If so, what technique(s) did the author employ to make it that way?

Grade 4 and up

- What is the book's text structure? Explain your rationale.
- What is the book's point of view? Explain your rationale.
- Does the author use comparisons? If so, give some examples. How do they help to make an idea easier to understand?
- Does the author use strong verbs? If so, give some examples. Why do you think they chose those verbs?
- Does the author use sensory details? If so, give some examples. Why do you think they included them?

Grade 5 and up

- Does the author use short sentences, long sentences, or a combination? How do the author's choices affect the way you read the text?

- Does the author include sentence fragments or questions in the text? If so, why do you think they made that choice?

- Does the author include exclamation points, parentheses, or dashes in the text? If so, why do you think they made that decision?

For middle school students, try this activity with excerpts of a long-form nonfiction book. After groups discuss some of the questions listed earlier, encourage them to look at individual sentences and paragraphs more carefully. The following questions can guide this examination of how nonfiction texts are constructed:

Grade 6 and up

- Does the author try to make examples in the text relevant to their readers' lives and experiences in the world? If so, give some examples. Why do you think the author employs this technique?

- Does the author use text scaffolding* to explain complex or abstract ideas? If so, give some examples.

- Does the author pack a lot of related information* into a single sentence? What are the advantages of doing this? What are the disadvantages?

- How can breaking a sentence into chunks* help readers understand it better? Provide some examples.

- How can recognizing organizational patterns in the text help you pinpoint important information? Provide some examples.

As the group discussions wind down, invite the teams to share their observations about craft elements in the book with the whole class. During this conversation, record the students' ideas on a piece of chart paper labeled "Examination." Then use those ideas to create a class list of key craft moves in the book you read aloud.

* See Chapter 5 for additional discussion of these terms and techniques.

When students have opportunities to practice identifying and evaluating the craftmanship in the nonfiction books they read, they'll intuitively begin to integrate these elements into their own writing. To make this process more transparent to your students, encourage them to identify the craft moves in their own expository writing and, if possible, specify a mentor author or mentor text that inspired them. For example, students might say something like, "I used a repetitive phrase in my writing like Cindy Jenson-Elliott did in *Weeds Find a Way*."

By now, we're confident that you realize the importance of exposing students to a rich array of nonfiction texts and are beginning to understand how utilizing the 5 Kinds of Nonfiction can help children as they read and write nonfiction. To help you gain a stronger sense of how this classification system can be applied to specific aspects of ELA instruction, the next three chapters will delve more deeply into nonfiction craft.

In our work with teachers and students, we've noticed that most K–8 educators feel confident teaching such nonfiction craft elements as compelling beginnings and satisfying endings but are eager to learn new instructional strategies for other key characteristics of nonfiction. To help meet that need, Chapter 5 focuses on text patterns as they pertain to text features, text format, and common sentence constructions. Patterns are also central to understanding text structures, but because text structure is such a critical nonfiction craft element, we're devoting an entire chapter—Chapter 6—to this topic. Chapter 7 discusses three important craft techniques that are a hallmark of high-quality fiction as well as nonfiction—voice and language, which are closely connected, as well as point of view. We think you'll be excited to try some of the ideas and activities we suggest in these upcoming chapters.

CHAPTER 5

Using the 5 Kinds of Nonfiction to Explore Text Patterns

"So many students are drawn to browseable books or active books as readers but often what we ask them to write in school doesn't look like these types of writing. Teaching students about the 5 Kinds of Nonfiction opens up options for critical thinking and choice in their own writing that will surely take writing workshop to the next level."

—Jen Vincent, language arts/social studies teacher, Carl Sandburg Middle School, Mundelein, Illinois

Patterns in Fiction and Nonfiction

A typical fiction story follows a pattern that we all know how to recognize. In fact, many preschool-aged children have already acquired the schema for the structure of a story (Stein and Glenn 1979).

In a story, a main character is placed in a particular setting. He or she faces a conflict, engages in actions to overcome a series of obstacles, and ultimately resolves the conflict, usually in a positive or satisfactory way. In most cases, the action proceeds in chronological order.

While narrative nonfiction generally follows a similar pattern, expository nonfiction is much more variable and versatile. There are so many different kinds of expository nonfiction, from a recipe scrawled on a napkin to a legal contract to a finely crafted children's book. Nevertheless, this style of writing still has patterns that students can learn to identify. And understanding those patterns can aid comprehension tremendously (Tovani 2000).

For example, every real estate contract is organized into sections, and those sections always appear in the same order. The same is true for marriage licenses, parking tickets, tax forms, and even a recipe. This uniformity makes key bits of information easier to locate and compare across texts.

The Power of Patterns: Text Features

In nonfiction picture books, words and illustrations work together to convey information.

In the same way, many nonfiction books for children, especially browseable nonfiction, traditional nonfiction, and expository literature, have standard text features that guide young readers. A book's table of contents, index, and headings help students locate specific information. A glossary helps readers understand unfamiliar words. Photos, illustrations, diagrams, and maps can help students understand key concepts and often deliver information more quickly and efficiently than words can. Yes, it's true, a picture really is worth a thousand words.

We're delighted that, in many schools, educators are currently introducing text features to K–2 students through strategies like a text feature walk. They're also encouraging students to identify and name common text features with activities like a text feature scavenger hunt. But in these lessons, teachers may be focusing exclusively on traditional nonfiction. We'd like to recommend doing these activities with browseable nonfiction and expository literature too.

We also suggest inviting early elementary students to use a wide range of nonfiction as mentor texts while creating text feature posters that showcase such visual text features as artwork with captions, diagrams with descriptive labels, and infographics. This will help children see that (1) in a nonfiction book, everything in the words *and* pictures has to be 100 percent true and (2) nonfiction authors spend a great deal of time developing visual text features that explain information clearly (Pike and Mumper 2004).

ACTIVITY 5.1

Text Feature Posters

After reading students a selection of age-appropriate books with a variety of visual text features, give each child an 11–by–17–inch piece of paper and art supplies. Invite the students to use words and pictures to create text feature posters about a topic you are currently studying or a topic of their choice using the text features in one of the books you shared as a mentor text. We recommend books in the following series:

- HarperCollins Let's Read and Find Out series (Choose titles published since 2015.)
- National Geographic Readers series
- Enslow Zoom in on Animals series

When the class seems ready, invite a few student volunteers to share their posters with the rest of the class.

During a classroom unit on bats, a first grader created this Compare & Contrast text feature poster with a fun close-up inset (left). A second grader was inspired to create a panda sidebar poster.

The Value of Think-Alouds

Throughout this chapter, we describe how recognizing patterns in expository nonfiction can aid students as they read and write. We've included a variety of activities to familiarize students with common patterns, but we'd also like to emphasize the role teacher think-alouds can play in helping students identify and understand these patterns.

As you read nonfiction aloud, we encourage you to model *how* patterns can support a reader's comprehension by making your thinking visible to your class. For example, as you're reading *Zoom in on Bees* by Melissa Stewart with younger students, you'll discover how a honeybee uses its eyes, antennae, wings, and legs. After reading about half of the book, you might pause and say: "Right now I have a question. I'm wondering if a young bee has all the same body parts as an adult. How can I find out if this book has the answer?"

If your students seemed stumped, point out that many nonfiction books have text features that can help readers find specific information. Flip to the front of the book and look at the table of contents. Flip to the back of the book and look at the index. They both indicate that young bees, or grubs, are discussed on page 21. You can turn to that page and read it right away or continue reading, knowing that your question will eventually be answered.

If you teach older students, you can use think-alouds to demonstrate how patterns in text formatting (see next section) and sentence construction (see page 72) are like trails of bread crumbs that nonfiction authors use to guide their readers.

The Power of Patterns: Text Format

In fiction and narrative nonfiction, text flows continuously from page to page, but in all four kinds of expository nonfiction, the text is often presented in distinct chunks. Why do authors format text in this way? Because it makes the text easier to read and understand. It encourages children to pause briefly, giving them a chance to digest the ideas and information.

In this browseable book, *Ick! Delightfully Disgusting Animal Dinners, Dwellings, and Defenses* by Melissa Stewart, the text is presented in discrete sections. After reading each one, children can pause and think.

The Dorling Kindersley designers and editors who developed the Eyewitness Books series back in the 1980s were the first to understand the incredible benefits of combining lavish illustrations with heavily formatted expository text. These books contain an astonishing amount of visual and written information, and yet the reader feels excited to explore rather than overwhelmed.

In addition, the uniform design of Eyewitness Books and the many other browseable books they've inspired is comforting to young readers, allowing them to easily locate and access information. The consistency also helps children compare similar content from page to page and book to book.

Intermediate students can easily identify formatting patterns in nonfiction books. The following activity can help them start to think about how words and images in a browseable book interact with one another on the printed page and why it's important for authors to carefully consider format during the writing process.

ACTIVITY 5.2

Text Format in Browseable Books*

After introducing *Eyewitness Books: Whales* by Vassili Papastavrou, place the book under a document camera and display it on your classroom interactive whiteboard. As you read the double-page spreads "Inside the whale" and "and baleen for filtering," encourage students to notice how the words and pictures in a browseable book work together to explain how a whale's body parts function and how they help the whale survive. You may wish to ask the following questions:

- What text features do you see on this double-page spread?

- Why do you think the author breaks the text into chunks?

- Why is some text larger and some text smaller?

*This activity directly addresses the Next Generation Science Standards Performance Expectation 4-LS1-1.

Next, divide the class into groups. After giving each team a copy of *Eyewitness Books: Whales* and an 11-by-17-inch piece of paper, introduce *Giant Squid* by Candace Fleming. Then place the book under a document camera and display it on your classroom

interactive whiteboard. Let your students know that they'll be using the information in this book to create a browseable book-style double-page spread that shows and describes an adult giant squid's key body parts.

TEACHING **TIP**

If you don't have a budget to buy multiple copies of the books we recommend for the activities in this book, work with your town librarian to obtain multiple copies through interlibrary loan. Most public libraries allow schools to keep books longer than the standard two weeks, and some are even willing to deliver books to nearby schools.

As you read *Giant Squid*, encourage students to take notes and create sketches in their writer's notebooks. If the children struggle with this task, model the process for a few double-page spreads by making notes and a quick sketch or two on chart paper. When you've finished reading the main text (but haven't shown the diagram at the end of the book), give the groups time to use their notes and sketches to create a browseable book-style double-page spread of the giant squid's key body parts. Encourage the teams to use *Eyewitness Books: Whales* as a mentor text during this process. (See sample on page 68).

If students find that they'd like to include information that isn't in the main text of the book, encourage them to record their unanswered questions in their writer's notebook. Ask students why they think the author decided not to include that information. Record any ideas they have on chart paper.

When the class seems ready, invite student volunteers to share their group's double-page spread with the rest of the class. During this time, you may wish to ask some of the following questions:

- What was the most challenging thing about this activity?
- How is the writing style in *Giant Squid* different from the writing style in *Eyewitness Books: Whales*?
- Why do you think the text in *Eyewitness Books: Whales* is more concise and straightforward?

- What differences do you notice in the language each author chooses?
- Why do you think the text in *Giant Squid* includes so many questions? Why are many of the sentences set on their own line rather than run together into a paragraph?

Now show students the diagram at the end of *Giant Squid*. You may wish to ask some of the following questions:

- How is this double-page spread similar to your browseable-style spread? How is it different?
- How is this double-page spread similar to the pages in *Eyewitness Books: Whales*? How is it different?
- Is the text on this double-page spread more straightforward than the rest of the book? If so, why do you think the author decided to write the text in this way?
- Does the text on this double-page spread include any information that is not on your browseable-style spread? If so, why didn't you include it?

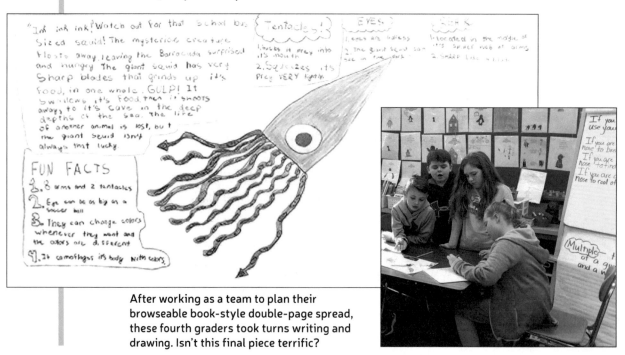

After working as a team to plan their browseable book-style double-page spread, these fourth graders took turns writing and drawing. Isn't this final piece terrific?

- Does the text on this double-page spread answer any of the questions you recorded in your writer's notebook? Why do you think the author decided to include this diagram in her book? (Because she thought readers might have specific questions about the giant squid's body features.)

After giving students time to update their browseable-style spreads using information in the *Giant Squid* diagram, bring this activity to a close by asking your class how they would categorize *Giant Squid* using the 5 Kinds of Nonfiction classification system.

Even though expository literature is rarely published in large series, it often includes text formatting patterns that help guide readers. For example, expository literature may feature dual-layer text, which consists of a short, simple main text that conveys main ideas and secondary text that provides supporting details.

As you read books like *Mama Built a Little Nest* by Jennifer Ward and *An Egg Is Quiet* by Dianna Hutts Aston, you will notice that the main text, which is set in larger type to let children know that they should read it first, can stand on its own and provide a general overview of the topic. It also captures the imagination of young readers, inspiring them to continue reading.

In Jess Keating's *Pink Is for Blobfish*, each double-page spread features four distinct text layers, and each one has a different type treatment to guide young readers in navigating the pages. Keating says she chose this multilayer approach to "give readers ownership over where they begin and how long they stay on each page."

Some children will "dive right in, get comfortable with the format, and never look up from a book until it's finished." Others may "dip their toes in first, not entirely sure if they want to continue."

With the recent popularity of graphic novels, it's no surprise that authors are now experimenting with nonfiction in a comics format. Many of these titles present information within the context of a storyline, but some, such as *How to Clean a Hippopotamus: A Look at Unusual Animal Partnerships* by Steve Jenkins and Robin Page, are entirely expository. The comics format is a good match for complex nonfiction topics because it's accessible and engaging, and the combination of words and images allows authors and illustrators to convey huge amounts of information on each spread. This format can also seamlessly integrate charts, diagrams, maps, and other visual text features.

In the following activity, intermediate students can take a close look at text formatting in expository literature and have an opportunity to consider how thinking about formatting helps nonfiction readers and writers.

Text Format in Expository Literature

To introduce students to various types of text formatting in expository literature, read aloud *Move!* by Steve Jenkins and Robin Page. Draw your students' attention to the verbs set in large type, the bold-faced animal names, and the ellipses (. . .) on each double-page spread. Point out that

each verb describes the movements of two animals, and two movements are described for each animal. Because this clever scheme moves readers from one spread to the next, the book's main idea is reinforced by the format.

Next, read aloud *Where in the Wild? Camouflaged Creatures Concealed . . . and Revealed* by David M. Schwartz and *Mama Built a Little Nest* by Jennifer Ward. Then guide your class in comparing the two books by asking the following questions:

- How is the format of the two books similar? How is it different?

- Does the poetic text in the two books perform the same function?

- Why do you think there is so much more descriptive text with supporting details in *Where in the Wild*?

- What do you think was each author's purpose for writing their book?

- Does the format of each book help the authors achieve their purpose? Explain your rationale.

To move these discussions from the whole class to smaller groups, share *An Egg Is Quiet* by Dianna Hutts Aston and *How to Clean a Hippopotamus: A Look at Unusual Animal Partnerships* by Steve Jenkins and Robin Page. Then divide the class into pairs or small groups and encourage each team to discuss the following questions:

Two third graders examining the format and visual text features in *An Egg Is Quiet* by Dianna Hutts Aston

- How is the format of the two books different? Are there any similarities in format?

- How does each author use visual text features?

- What do you think was each author's purpose for writing their book?

- Does the format of each book help the authors achieve their purpose? Explain your rationale.

As the group discussions wind down, encourage each team to share its ideas with the rest of the class.

The Power of Patterns: Interruption Construction

Let's face it. Even when students are engaged, reading nonfiction can be challenging. After all, students have to do more than just follow the actions of characters in a story. They have to develop an understanding of the content, and in many cases, the information and ideas are brand new to them.

As children begin to read middle-grade titles, the text becomes increasingly complex. In all 5 Kinds of Nonfiction, sentences are often jam-packed with information that takes time and close reading to synthesize and interpret. The good news is that the information is often presented in patterns, and when students know how to identify those patterns, they can break sentences into more manageable chunks.

When writers use the interruption construction, they insert a bit of extra information between commas or em dashes (Fang 2006; Wheeler-Topen 2019). You can easily teach students to recognize this type of dependent clause using the example on page 4 of *Snowy Owl Invasion!: Tracking an Unusual Migration* by Sandra Markle:

> "On one sand dune, peeking through winter-dried plants, sat a big white bird—a snowy owl."

After writing this sentence on the classroom whiteboard, cover the interrupting phrase "peeking through winter-dried plants" with your hand to show students that the remaining parts of the sentence form a complete thought.

Let your class know that if a sentence like this seems overwhelming to them, they can cover the interruption with their finger. After they understand the main part of the sentence, they can read the phrase to get some bonus information. In the example above, the interruption provides a lovely detail that helps readers visualize the owl in their minds.

Here's another example from page 11 of *Itch! Everything You Didn't Want to Know About What Makes You Scratch* by Anita Sanchez:

> "Parasites are organisms that use other living things—like you and me—for food and shelter."

In this case, the interruption helps to make the reader feel more connected to the content.

ACTIVITY 5.4

Interruption Construction Treasure Hunt*

To give students practice interacting with the interruption construction, divide the class into small groups and pass out copies of *Death Eaters: Meet Nature's Scavengers* by Kelly Milner Halls. Encourage the teams to find as many examples as they can of the interruption construction. (If students struggle with this activity, suggest that they try page 18.) Ask teammates to use a sticky note to mark each example and write a quick explanation of why the author employed this writing technique. How does each extra bit of information enrich the writing?

When the groups seem ready, invite student volunteers to share one of the examples their team found and the reason they think the author decided to use the interruption construction in this location. Classmates should feel free to agree or respectfully disagree with the presenter. They may also ask questions or offer their own insights.

Finally, invite students to look back at nonfiction they wrote earlier in the year. Can they find any places where they used the interruption construction? If not, encourage them to hunt for one or two spots where they could add this sentence construction and then revise their piece.

The Moon

If you want to know some facts about the moon then you have come to the right expert. The moon has gray dust called moon dust on it. On the moon you wouldn't need a bathing suit because there isn't a lot of water. Scientists did find evidence of ice, so that could mean some water. The moon doesn't have an atmosphere, it's actually called an exosphere, and so there isn't any weather there either. The moon does have craters, bowl shaped holes like pits, made by meteor showers. Astronauts who travel to the moon have to know there isn't a lot of gravity and they will feel lighter than on earth. Just like earth, the moon has mountains, valleys and plains. I think it is an interesting place. I hope astronauts and scientists learn more exciting facts about the moon by studying it for a long, long, time.

A fourth grader spotted two examples of the interruption construction in a piece she wrote about the moon.

---

*This activity supports Next Generation Science Standards Performance Expectation 5-LS2-1.

The Power of Patterns: Text Scaffolding

Another pattern that students can hunt for in all 5 Kinds of Nonfiction is text scaffolding. As you probably know, when teachers use instructional scaffolding, they give students support in gradually learning a new skill or concept. In the same way, an author can provide support to help readers understand a complex idea (Pusey 2018).

Because children have limited prior knowledge and may have trouble thinking abstractly, nonfiction books often include clusters of sentences that slowly build an explanation. Authors start by meeting readers where they are. Then they craft a series of connected sentences that act like building blocks to guide students in gradually developing an understanding of the concept.

On page 7 of *Super Gear: Nanotechnology and Sports Team Up*, author Jennifer Swanson deftly employs text scaffolding to explain why nanomaterials have a large surface area. Swanson begins by clearly defining the term *surface area,* in case it's new to her readers. Next, she uses an everyday example (a potato being cut into french fries) to show how surface area increases as an item (the potato) is cut into smaller and smaller pieces. She then forges a connection between this example and nanoparticles, which are like billions

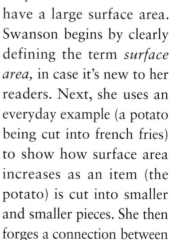

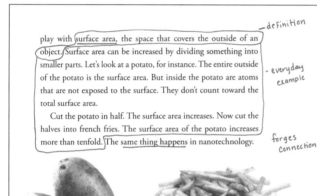

— definition

play with surface area, the space that covers the outside of an object. Surface area can be increased by dividing something into smaller parts. Let's look at a potato, for instance. The entire outside of the potato is the surface area. But inside the potato are atoms that are not exposed to the surface. They don't count toward the total surface area.

- everyday example

Cut the potato in half. The surface area increases. Now cut the halves into french fries. The surface area of the potato increases more than tenfold. The same thing happens in nanotechnology.

forges connection

A whole potato has less surface area than the same potato cut into slices or french fries, because more of it is underneath the surface.

nanomaterial description

A nanomaterial can be made up of billions and billions of nanoparticles. The outside of each nanoparticle counts toward the total surface area. This gives the nanomaterial a much greater surface area than that of a normal substance. The larger surface area allows for more interaction between particles. Now instead of just two larger particles interacting with each other, you may have ten nanoparticles sticking together. The extra interactions can speed up a reaction or improve the strength and durability of a product.

Tiny Bits of Science   7

and billions of itty-bitty potato pieces. Finally, she describes how these billions of pieces give the nanomaterial a much greater surface area than that of a regular substance.

Because Swanson's precisely worded sentences build one upon another, step-by-step, readers feel supported as they move from one idea to the next and, ultimately, gain a clear and accurate understanding of the complex information.

ACTIVITY 5.5

Text Scaffolding Treasure Hunt*

To help students understand how text scaffolding works, use a document camera to display page 7 of the expository literature title *Super Gear: Nanotechnology and Sports Team Up* on your classroom interactive whiteboard and show students the steps Jennifer Swanson uses to help readers build an understanding of why nanomaterials have a large surface area.

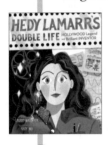 

Next, divide the class into small groups and pass out copies of the narrative nonfiction titles *Hedy Lamarr's Double Life: Hollywood Legend and Brilliant Inventor* by Laurie Wallmark and *Mario and the Hole in the Sky: How a Chemist Saved Our Planet* by Elizabeth Rusch. Encourage each team to spend time reading and examining their book carefully. Let the students know that they may need to read passages multiple times before they're able to identify instances of text scaffolding. As they spot examples, they should mark them with a sticky note and make a few notes about the concept being explained.

*This activity supports the Next Generation Science Standards Performance Expectations 4-PS3-2, 4-PS4-1, and MS-PS1-2.

When all the groups have completed this task, invite student volunteers to share one of the scaffolding examples their team found and the concept it clarifies. Classmates should feel free to agree or respectfully disagree with the presenter. They may also ask questions or offer their own insights. To facilitate the conversation and promote full-class engagement, help students stay focused on the topic. Restate any unclear comments or ideas and encourage students to give one another the time they need to formulate and express their ideas and rationale.

As students have opportunities to think about and explore the patterns of nonfiction we've discussed in this chapter, they'll become more capable and confident readers and writers. But it's also important for them to gain a deep understanding of the most critical nonfiction organizational pattern of all—text structure. For that reason, we've devoted all of Chapter 6 to this key craft element.

6

Using the 5 Kinds of Nonfiction to Explore Text Structures

"Every topic can be approached in numerous different ways. Before writers can settle on a text structure, they must figure out what they most want to say, and then pick the approach that says it best."

—Brenda Z. Guiberson, award-winning children's book author

Text Structures in Reading

Nonfiction authors use text structure to arrange and connect ideas. When readers know how to identify these organizational patterns, they can access, understand, and remember the information more easily (Englert and Hibert 1984; Horowitz 1985a; Horowitz 1985b; McGee and Richgels 1985; Piccolo 1987; Akhondi, Malayeri, and Samad 2011).

Many educators teach nonfiction text structure at the sentence level, but we'd like to encourage teachers to put more emphasis on discussing the overall text structure of the books students read. Most traditional nonfiction and browseable nonfiction books have a Description text structure, active nonfiction generally features a Sequence structure, and nearly all narrative nonfiction has a Chronological Sequence structure, but expository literature can have just about any text structure you can think of. Here are some of our favorite books from each of the five text structure categories espoused by state ELA standards:

DESCRIPTION

The Frog Book by Steve Jenkins

Many: The Diversity of Life on Earth by Nicola Davies

Bonkers About Beetles by Owen Davey

A Hundred Billion Trillion Stars by Seth Fishman

SEQUENCE

Bugged: How Insects Changed History by Sarah Albee

How to Swallow a Pig: Step-by-Step Advice from the Animal Kingdom by Steve Jenkins and Robin Page

Trout Are Made of Trees by April Pulley Sayre

We Are Grateful: Otsaliheliga by Traci Sorell

COMPARE & CONTRAST

Big & Little by Steve Jenkins

Daylight Starlight Wildlife by Wendell Minor

Birds of a Feather: Bowerbirds and Me by Susan L. Roth

Rodent Rascals by Roxie Munro

CAUSE & EFFECT

Earth: Feeling the Heat by Brenda Z. Guiberson

If Sharks Disappeared by Lily Williams

If You Hopped Like a Frog by David M. Schwartz

Never Smile at a Monkey: And 17 Other Important Things to Remember by Steve Jenkins

PROBLEM-SOLUTION

Boy, Were We Wrong About Dinosaurs! by Kathleen Kudlinksi

The Great Monkey Rescue: Saving the Golden Lion Tamarins by Sandra Markle

Mesmerized: How Ben Franklin Solved a Mystery That Baffled All of France by Mara Rockliff

She Persisted: 13 American Women Who Changed the World by Chelsea Clinton

When discussing nonfiction books for children, we think it's also important to call attention to two additional text structures, which are quite common—List and Question & Answer (Pike and Mumper 2004; Siu-Ruyan 1998).

In a "List book," the main idea is presented on the first double-page spread. Then each subsequent spread offers one or more examples that support that idea. In many cases, a List book has a concluding spread that links back to the opening or offers a fun twist on the topic, leaving readers with a sense of satisfaction. A List text structure works especially well for books that focus on plant or animal characteristics, adaptations, or behaviors. Here are some of our favorite examples:

LIST

Look at Me! How to Attract Attention in the Animal World by Steve Jenkins

Homes in the Wild: Where Baby Animals and Their Parents Live by Lita Judge

Pink Is for Blobfish: Discovering the World's Perfectly Pink Animals by Jess Keating

This Is How We Do It: One Day in the Lives of Seven Kids from Around the World by Matt LaMothe

TEACHING **TIP**

Q&A books are perfect for classroom transitions because students are captivated by the information. The chunks of text are short and manageable but meaningful at the same time. If you teach elementary school, you can read a few pages of a Q&A book at the end of morning meeting, while waiting for the buses to be called, or any other time you want to sneak in a little additional reading (and learning).

We find it surprising that state ELA standards do not include Question & Answer in their list of sample text structures. Not only is Q&A a powerful way to organize information, it also provides multiple entry points to the content and can add a fun, interactive gamelike quality to a book. And that's not all. Because the Q&A format is easy for even young children to identify, it's a great window into text structures, allowing students to get their feet wet before immersing themselves in text structures that are more difficult to grasp and differentiate. On the next page are some of our favorite examples.

QUESTION & ANSWER

Bone by Bone: Comparing Animal Skeletons by Sara Levine

Do Sharks Glow in the Dark? . . . and Other Shark-tastic Questions by Mary Kay Carson

Hatch! by Roxie Munro

What Do You Do with a Tail Like This? by Steve Jenkins and Robin Page

ACTIVITY 6.1

Introducing Text Structures with Q&A

A week or two before you plan to do this activity, create a Wonder Wall bulletin board in your classroom. When students return from recess or have a few extra minutes, invite them to write questions about things that make them curious on sticky notes and add them to the Wonder Wall.

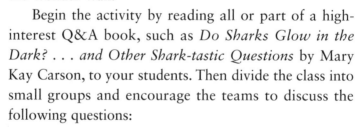

Begin the activity by reading all or part of a high-interest Q&A book, such as *Do Sharks Glow in the Dark? . . . and Other Shark-tastic Questions* by Mary Kay Carson, to your students. Then divide the class into small groups and encourage the teams to discuss the following questions:

- How does the author use questions and answers to organize the information she wants to share with readers?

- Why do you think the author structured her text in this way? Do you see any advantages?

When the groups seem ready, invite a few student volunteers to share their team's thoughts. Classmates should feel free to agree or respectfully disagree with the presenter. They may also ask questions or offer their own insights.

Next, invite the teams to look for three or four questions on the classroom Wonder Wall that have something in common and write them on a separate piece of paper. How could these questions be used to create a Q&A book with a common topic or idea? Encourage the groups to arrange the questions in an order that makes sense to them and come up with a possible title for their book.

Let your class know that nonfiction writers often use recognizable structures to organize their text. One popular text structure is Question & Answer. Other common text structures include Compare & Contrast and Cause & Effect. As you explain the characteristics of these two text structures, list these features as well as important signal words on separate pieces of chart paper. Next, read a few pages of *If You Hopped Like a Frog* by David M. Schwartz and a few pages of *Birds of a Feather: Bowerbirds and Me* by Susan L. Roth.

After letting your class know that one of these books has a predominant Compare & Contrast text structure and the other has a predominant Cause & Effect text structure, invite students to turn and talk with a neighbor about which book has each structure. Encourage students to review the characteristics you listed on chart paper as they make their decision. When the buddy conversations wind down, ask a few student volunteers to share their thinking. You may wish to add some of their ideas to the chart paper lists.

When you're confident that students understand why *Birds of a Feather: Bowerbirds and Me* has a predominant Compare & Contrast text structure and *If You Hopped Like a Frog* has a predominant Cause & Effect text structure, divide the class into small groups. Pass out copies of *If You Hopped Like a Frog* to half of the groups

---

TEACHING **TIP**

During these discussions, some students might argue that *If You Hopped Like a Frog* has characteristics of a List text structure as well as a Compare & Contrast text structure. We agree with them! But we classify it as predominantly Cause & Effect because it contains repeated if-then statements.

and *Birds of a Feather: Bowerbirds and Me* to the rest of the teams. Encourage each team to create a text structure map (similar to the one shown below) that visually represents their book's text structure by summarizing the information on each double page spread and highlighting the signal words. Let your students know that a graphic organizer, such as a text structure map, is often the best way to identify and understand the overall text structure of a nonfiction book.

TEXT Structure Mapping If you Hopped Like a Frog

If people had the same jumping ability as' frogs, they would be able to leap to first base.	If we had the same strength for our body size as an ant you would be able to lift a car.	If you had the same size brain as the brachiosaurus, your brain would be smaller than a pea	If you swallowed like a snake you would be able to gulp down a hotdog thicker than a telephone pole
If people ate like a shrew they could eat 700 hamburgers in one day	If you had the same jump as a flea you could jump as far and high as the lady liberty's torch	If you had a chameleon tongue you could whip food off a plate without your hands	If you had a Crane's neck you would have to stretch up high to scratch your head
If you had eagle eyes you could see a rabbit from the clouds	If you ate like a Pelican you could drink three floats in one mouthfull.	If you grew as fast in your first nine months as before you were born you would be heavier than 2 million elephants	If you moved like spiders you could run the entire football field in two seconds

The text structure is <u>Cause</u> and <u>effect</u> because each part explains that if you had the same size proportion or ability as a certain Creature then the effect would be what you could do or the size of something you would have

Creating a text structure map for *If You Hopped Like a Frog* by David M. Schwartz and highlighting signal words allowed a fifth grader to visualize the book's predominant text structure.

ACTIVITY 6.2

Same Topic, Different Text Structures*

To give students practice identifying and comparing text structures in the books they read, divide your class into seven groups and give each team one of the following books:

Fanatical About Frogs by Owen Davey (Description)

Frog or Toad? How Do You Know? by Melissa Stewart (Compare & Contrast)

Frogs by Nic Bishop (Description)

Frog Song by Brenda Z. Guiberson (List)

The Hidden Life of a Toad by Doug Weschler (Sequence)

A Place for Frogs by Melissa Stewart (main text = Cause & Effect, sidebars = Problem-Solution)

Red-Eyed Tree Frog by Joy Cowley (Sequence)

Invite each group to examine and read portions of their book, identify its text structure, and make a list of the kinds of information the author would have had to research to write the book. When all the teams have completed this task, ask each group to rotate to a different station, taking their lists with them but leaving the books behind, and repeat the process. After the teams have reviewed all the books, encourage the groups to share and compare their lists.

Do the teams agree about the text structure of each book? Some students will probably classify *A Place for Frogs* as Cause & Effect, while others may classify it as Problem-Solution. Ask the groups to

---

*This activity supports Next Generation Science Standards Performance Expectations 3-LS1-1, 3-LS4-4, 4-LS1-1, and 5-LS2-1.

explain their rationale. During the discussion, guide students in realizing that a book can have more than one major text structure. In the case of *A Place for Frogs,* the main text has a Cause & Effect structure, whereas the sidebars have a Problem-Solution structure.

Ask students why they think the author decided to use two different structures. (The main text provides general ideas and is written in a way that helps readers realize that their actions can have a positive impact on the animals that share our world. The sidebars support the main text by highlighting ways scientists and community members have worked together to protect wildlife and wild places.)

Next, ask the class if any of the books they reviewed had the same text structure. (*Fanatical About Frogs* by Owen Davey and *Frogs* by Nic Bishop both have a Description text structure. *The Hidden Life of a Toad* by Doug Weschler and *Red-Eyed Tree Frog* by Joy Cowley both have a Sequence text structure.) How are the books in each set similar? How are they different? In each case, did the students prefer one book over the other? Encourage students to explain their rationale. Do the books in each set have much overlapping information?

Finally, point out that *Frog or Toad? How Do You Know?* and *A Place for Frogs* were written by the same author. Then ask the class if they think Melissa Stewart used the same body of research to write the two books. (No, there is almost no overlapping information.) This is a great opportunity to point out that text structure often dictates the kinds of information authors need to collect as they do research. When a writer chooses a text structure early in the process, it can make the research process more focused and efficient.

Text Structures in Writing

One of the greatest challenges a nonfiction writer faces is finding just the right text structure. While most books have one of the seven text structures discussed earlier, some have a text structure that echoes the content. For example, in *Swirl by Swirl: Spirals in Nature,* Joyce Sidman employs a clever Ladder text structure. The book begins with examples of

spiraling objects that are small and snug, such as a nautilus shell and a chipmunk curled up underground in winter. As the text progresses, the examples slowly grow and stretch and unfurl—a wave, a hurricane, a galaxy. Then, as the end of the book approaches, the examples gradually shrink in scale and curl up tight again.

In *The Next President: The Unexpected Beginnings and Unwritten Future of America's Presidents,* Kate Messner uses an innovative Chain Reaction text structure to highlight that at any given time in U.S. history, there is one president running the country and many future presidents preparing for their role—even though they don't know it. And, in fact, right now—today—there are at least ten future presidents alive in the United States. They might be playing basketball or drawing a picture, solving math problems or even reading a book about U.S. presidents. What a wonderful way to empower kids!

Even when using standard text structures, nonfiction authors find an amazing variety of ways to share the ideas and information they're passionate about. For example, *Lincoln and Kennedy: A Pair to Compare* by Gene Barretta and *Rodent Rascals* by Roxie Munro both have Compare & Contrast text structures, but the way the two titles make use of that structure is quite different.

In Barretta's book, each left-hand page presents facts about Abraham Lincoln, while the facing right-hand page offers corresponding information about John F. Kennedy. As a result, readers notice fun patterns as well as startling similarities between the two men's lives. The book's ending forges a connection with readers by introducing the term "legacy" and asking children to think about how they plan to exist in the world.

In contrast, *Rodent Rascals* invites young readers to compare twenty-one fascinating rodents—from chipmunks to naked mole rats to beavers—with charming art that shows them at their actual size and brief descriptions that highlight some of their most interesting characteristics and behaviors.

We like to compare searching for a text structure to shopping for a pair of pants. When we shop for pants, we usually know what purpose we want them to serve. Are they for playing sports? Relaxing around the house? Going to a fancy party? Keeping their purpose in mind allows us to eliminate some pants pretty quickly. We can also rule out pants if they're the wrong size or a color we don't like. But at a certain point, we have to try on a few pairs of pants to see how they fit.

The same is true for selecting a nonfiction text structure. When writers consider their purpose for writing, identify their audience, and decide exactly what they're most excited to share with readers, they can quickly eliminate some text structures. For example, a Sequence structure won't work if the topic lacks a time element or natural order. A Compare & Contrast structure works only if the author is discussing or evaluating two different objects, creatures, or ideas.

But like shopping for a pair of pants, at a certain point, a writer often has to try on a couple of different text structures to see which one fits best. When Melissa was writing *Can an Aardvark Bark?*, she experimented with four different text structures before finally deciding that a Question & Answer text structure would work best. To learn more about Melissa's four-year journey to find the best text structure, you can watch the videos shown in Figure 6.1 via the URL: www.melissa-stewart.com/timelines/timeline_aardvark/timeline _aardvark.html or by using the QR code on the left.

FIGURE 6.1 Searching for a Text Structure

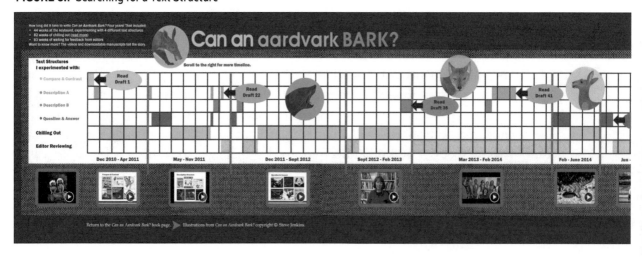

According to Caldecott Honor-winning author-illustrator Steve Jenkins, "the text structure for a book usually emerges as I'm doing research, making notes, and writing early drafts of a manuscript." But sometimes the perfect structure is obvious from the start.

"*Never Smile at a Monkey: And 17 Other Important Things to Remember* was inspired by that phrase popping into my head when I read that macaques sometimes react violently to a human smile (a display of teeth)," recalls Jenkins. "From the beginning, I knew that I'd base the book on a series of similar admonitions (never clutch a cane toad, never cuddle a cub, never touch a tang)." Because Jenkins planned to discuss many different creatures, he knew immediately that he'd be writing a List book.

Getting to Know Author Steve Jenkins

As you read through the book titles on pages 79–82, you may have noticed that one author—Steve Jenkins—has a book included in each of the seven text structure categories. As far as we're concerned, Jenkins should be crowned the King of Expository Literature.

Most of Jenkins's books are about animals and all the cool ways they survive in the world. The consistent cut-paper art style gives the books a unified look that immediately lets you know he's the creator. And yet every book is distinctive because he's constantly experimenting with the way he employs various craft elements, especially text structure.

Some teachers already do author studies of Steve Jenkins, but we think *every* student should study Jenkins's titles closely as they learn to identify text structures in the books they read and integrate text structures into their writing.

Award-winning author Brenda Z. Guiberson agrees that sometimes the perfect text structure for a book is obvious to her right away, but other times, she says, it's a real struggle. For example, she knew that *Feathered Dinosaurs* "would be a List book from the very beginning," but "it took a long time, and several false starts" to find the right predominant structure for *Earth: Feeling the Heat.*

"I was trying to say too much about a complicated global issue," Guiberson explains. "Finally, I decided to stick with specific details and let the situations speak for themselves. Then it became a Cause & Effect book."

Just like professional writers, young writers should have opportunities to think carefully about text structure during the prewriting process. They should also understand that "trying on" different text structures is an authentic part of the drafting process. The following activity can help students (1) understand how various text structures are related to one another and (2) develop the skills necessary to efficiently and effectively toggle back and forth between text structures.

ACTIVITY 6.3

Experimenting with Text Structures

After reading *What Do You Do with a Tail Like This?* by Steve Jenkins and Robin Page to students, divide the class into small groups and invite each team to make a text structure map (see page 84), so they can get a stronger sense of how the book's main text structure (Question & Answer) and its secondary text structure (Cause & Effect) work together. Then encourage each child to choose a four-page section and rewrite the text with a Problem-Solution text structure.

If students struggle with this activity, you may wish to work through an example with them. The section about noses includes the following text:

What do you do with a nose like this?

If you're a platypus, you use your nose to dig in the mud.

If you're a hyena, you find your next meal with your nose.

If you're an elephant, you use your nose to give yourself a bath.

If you're a mole, you use your nose to find your way underground.

If you're an alligator, you breathe through your nose while hiding underwater.

Invite students to identify the problem the hyena is facing. Once they realize that the hyena needs to find its next meal, encourage them to turn the text around so that the problem comes first and the solution comes second. Their rewritten text featuring a Problem-Solution text structure might look like this:

A platypus needs to dig in the mud. What body part does it use?

A hyena needs to find its next meal. What body part does it use?

An elephant needs to give itself a bath. What body part does it use?

A mole needs to find its way underground. What body part does it use?

An alligator needs to breathe while it's hiding underwater. What body part does it use?

Its nose!

After reading *What Do You Do with a Tail Like This?*, these fifth graders rewrote Steve Jenkins's text using a Problem-Solution text structure.

A bat needs to see.
What body part does it use?

A jack rabbit needs to keep cool.
What body part does it use?

An underwater hippo needs to close off water from sleeping in.
What body part does it use?

A cricket needs to hear.
What body part does it use?

A humpack whale needs to hear sounds hun of miles away.
What body part does it use?

Its Ears!

When students have completed this task using the four-page section of their choice, they may wish to illustrate their writing. If time permits, invite a few student volunteers to share their work with the class.

ACTIVITY 6.4

Same Text Structure, New Topic*

After completing Activity 6.3, begin this multiday activity by sharing a variety of books about how animals use various body parts. We recommend the books in the What If You Had series by Sandra Markle (Scholastic) and the Animal Bodies Up Close series by Melissa Stewart (Enslow).

* This activity directly addresses the Next Generation Science Standards Performance Expectation 4-LS1-1.

After reading two books on the same topic, such as animal ears, invite your class to compare the craft elements in the two books. Ask them the following questions:

- How is the art similar? How is it different?
- What text features do you notice in each book?
- How is the writing style in the two books similar? How is it different?
- What text structure did each author use?
- How is each of these books different from *What Do You Do with a Tail Like This?* by Steve Jenkins and Robin Page?

During this process, it may help to read portions of the books under a document camera.

Next, let your students know that they're going to use the information in the books you've provided to write their own book about the animal body part of their choice using a Problem-Solution text structure.[†]

We suggest students include an introduction, three or four animal examples, and a conclusion. The books should also feature a table of contents and a list of sources. Students may add a glossary if they think it would be useful to readers.

The children may illustrate their books with either drawings or photos. If students don't have experience searching for photos, inserting them, and including credit for the source of the photos, be ready to support them through this process.

An animal example page created by a fourth grader who decided to focus on animal teeth.

[†] In some cases, students may wish to do additional research with an online encyclopedic database, such as PebbleGo.

When the project is complete, arrange for your students to share their books with one or more other classes at your school. Then invite students to add their books to the school library. The books should be integrated into the collection, so anyone interested in animal body parts has an opportunity to read the students' books.

As students experiment with text structures using finely crafted children's literature as mentors, they'll come to understand that the authors of these books are like ranchers attempting to control and corral their herd. By using organizational patterns to manage and manipulate the way ideas and information are presented, authors make the content as clear and engaging as possible (Flood, Lapp, and Farnan 1986).

Why do children's book authors put so much careful craftsmanship into their work? Why do they care so deeply about helping readers understand? Because they're passionate about their topic, and they're excited to share what they've discovered. While the main purpose of a newspaper reporter or a textbook author may be to inform, that's not enough for authors of high-quality nonfiction books (Bamford and Kristo 1998; Short and Armstrong 1993). They strive to delight, to captivate, to inspire their audience. And young readers can absolutely tell the difference.

While it's important for students to understand text structures and other craft elements unique to nonfiction, it's also valuable for them to have experience identifying and practicing craft moves that fiction and nonfiction have in common. With that goal in mind, Chapter 7 takes a close look at how a strong voice, rich language, and carefully chosen point of view can enrich nonfiction writing.

Using the 5 Kinds of Nonfiction to Explore Voice, Language, and Point of View

"Looking more closely at the different kinds of nonfiction helps students think critically about how nonfiction can be written in different ways. Not only does this help students as readers but it gives them a construct to think through when writing nonfiction as well."

—Jen Vincent, language arts/social studies teacher,
Carl Sandburg Middle School, Mundelein, Illinois

Commercial Nonfiction vs. Literary Nonfiction

We'd like to begin this chapter by inviting you to take another look at the 5 Kinds of Nonfiction visual that we shared in Chapter 2. The order of the five categories in Figure 7.1—active, browseable, traditional, expository literature, narrative—is no accident. It highlights that active nonfiction and browseable nonfiction have more in common with each other than they do with expository literature and narrative nonfiction and vice versa.

Both adult and children's trade publishers divide fiction and nonfiction books into two broad categories—commercial and literary. Commercial fiction, written by such authors as Mary Higgins Clark, Gordon Korman, Stephen King, Mary Pope Osborne, James Patterson, and Lauren Tarshis, has mass appeal, and editors expect it to make a substantial profit. These books are fast paced with strong plots and limited characterization. Their themes are usually fairly obvious, and the language and syntax aren't too complex.

In contrast, literary fiction, written by such authors as Kate DiCamillo, Toni Morrison, Joyce Carol Oates, John Updike, Padma Venkatraman, and Jacqueline Woodson, is more likely to receive starred reviews and win awards. These books feature rich,

FIGURE 7.1 5 Kinds of Nonfiction

Active · Browseable · Traditional · Expository Literature · Narrative

Commercial Nonfiction · Literary Nonfiction

multifaceted stories with well-developed characters, lush language, and complex, timeless themes.

Similarly, commercial nonfiction for children has mass appeal. These active and browseable titles generally sell well in bookstores and mass market outlets (like Target and Walmart) with some crossover to schools and libraries. Literary nonfiction for children, on the other hand, is more likely to win awards and is considered higher-quality writing. These expository literature and narrative nonfiction titles sell primarily to schools and libraries with some crossover to bookstores and, occasionally, to mass market outlets.

How Traditional Nonfiction Fits In

While both commercial and literary nonfiction are purchased by schools and libraries, a third segment of the children's book market caters specifically to these "institutional" customers. Publishers like Rosen, Lerner, and Capstone all produce large series of traditional nonfiction books with clear, concise, straightforward text and a standard design. Because they're written quickly and must adhere to specific guidelines (reading level, page design, curricular standards, word count, etc.), these titles often aren't as finely crafted as literary nonfiction or as dynamically designed as commercial nonfiction. Nevertheless, they do have one major advantage—they provide age-appropriate information on just about any topic you can think of.

Why is this so important? Because the best way— sometimes the only way—to turn an info-kid into a reader is by handing them a book on a topic they find fascinating. A child who's passionate about monster trucks may toss aside a finely crafted book about the history of automobiles, but if you give that child a traditional nonfiction title all about monster trucks, they'll devour it and ask for more. When teachers and librarians understand and respect all 5 Kinds of Nonfiction, they're better equipped to help a broad range of children find true texts they'll love.

When educators use the term "literary nonfiction," they're (understandably) thinking more about craft elements than sales potential. According to *The Fountas & Pinnell Literacy Continuum*, literary nonfiction is "a nonfiction text that employs literary techniques, such as figurative language, to present information in engaging ways" (Fountas and Pinnell 2016).

Because current state ELA standards are closely aligned with the Common Core State Standards (even in states that never adopted CCSS), it's worth looking at that document too. It lists the following as examples of literary nonfiction (NGAC and CCSSO 2010):

- Some personal essays and speeches
- Most biographies/autobiographies
- Memoirs
- Narrative nonfiction*
- Some poetry
- Some informational picture books

Why does the 5 Kinds of Nonfiction classification system make a point of differentiating between commercial categories (active and browseable) and literary categories (expository literature and narrative)? Because one of its goals is to give authors, editors, agents, book reviewers, awards committee members, librarians, literacy educators, and classroom teachers a common lexicon for discussing the wide and wonderful world of nonfiction for kids. Only then can publishers understand the kinds of nonfiction books that ALL students want and need.

Because most children's book editors gravitate toward narratives, publishers are currently putting a lot of emphasis on narrative nonfiction. We hope they will soon become aware of the research showing that many young readers prefer expository nonfiction and realize that four out of the five categories in the 5 Kinds of Nonfiction classification

---

*It's interesting that the Common Core differentiates life stories (biographies, autobiographies, and memoirs) from narrative nonfiction. In the children's literature community, picture book biographies are considered quintessential examples of narrative nonfiction.

system have an expository writing style.

And based on that knowledge, we hope publishers will (1) begin acquiring more expository literature, especially books about social studies/history and the arts as well as titles on any topic written and illustrated by people from traditionally marginalized com-

Author Sarah Albee celebrates the publication of her innovative browseable nonfiction title *North America: A Fold-Out Graphic History* with a class of fifth graders.

munities, and (2) look for creative ways to incorporate what kids love about active and browseable nonfiction into books with the elements of finely crafted prose. These craft elements include innovative text structure, which we discussed in Chapter 6, as well as three techniques that literary fiction and literary nonfiction have in common—strong voice, rich language, and carefully chosen point of view. This trifecta is discussed in detail below.

The Voice Choice

At one time, children's book editors rejected nonfiction manuscripts with a strong, distinct voice. They believed that the information, not the presentation, should be the major attraction. But today, voice is recognized as an important element of literary nonfiction.

What exactly is voice? Educators generally describe voice as the "personality of the writing" or "how the writing makes the reader feel." These definitions may help readers gain a stronger sense of how to identify voice in a text, but they don't help writers as they're trying to craft it. That's why we prefer the astonishingly clear, simple definition developed by Newbery-award-winning author Linda Sue Park:

voice = word choice + rhythm

Park defines "rhythm" in an equally clear and simple way:

rhythm = punctuation + sentence length

Not only does this brilliant equation apply to voice in both fiction and nonfiction, it also makes a craft move that often seems mysterious and elusive instantly manageable. After all, word choice, punctuation, and sentence length are all easy to control, easy to vary, easy to play around with (Park 2019).

Tone vs. Voice

Tone is about the writer. It's what you hear when you read a personal narrative, an opinion piece, or a personal letter. For example, if a child gets a broken toy for their birthday, they might write a complaint letter to the toy company. The tone of the letter would be frustrated and angry because that's how the child feels. Their feelings come through loud and clear in the writing.

Voice is about the reader. An author crafts the experience they want the reader to have. A writer may not be feeling so lively on days when they're working on a manuscript with a lively voice. But they have chosen that voice because the writer thinks it's the best way to share the topic with readers.

As you can see in Figure 7.2, nonfiction voice options span a continuum, from lively to lyrical with plenty of choices in between. Writers select a voice based on their topic and their purpose for writing (Moss 2003).

In *Itch! Everything You Didn't Want to Know About What Makes You Scratch,* author Anita Sanchez deftly employs a humorous, conversational voice. Here's a short excerpt from a sidebar with the playful title "Lice Advice."

> If you do find out you're hosting lice, don't freak out! Hair lice don't spread disease or cause serious health problems. Still, you don't want insects using your head for a habitat. See your doctor to find out how to get rid of unwanted company.

FIGURE 7.2 The Nonfiction Voice Continuum

Lively   # Lyrical

goofy   playful   light, lovely
irreverent   stately, respectful
sassy   calm, cozy
passionate, excited   soothing
humorous   confessional   wondrous
conversational   descriptive

By choosing fun word combinations like "freak out" and "unwanted company" and including the alliterative phrase "head for a habitat" as well as the exclamation point at the end of the first sentence, Sanchez crafts text that delights as well as informs. Even though all four sentences are about the same length, the author has varied the sentence structure to make the passage fast paced.

Now consider the opening lines of *Giant Squid* by Candace Fleming, which has a more wondrous, lyrical voice.

Down,
   down,
  in the depths
   of the sunless sea
    deep,
     deep
   in the cold,
    cold dark,
     creatures,
    strange
      and fearsome.
     lurk.

This text may occupy twelve lines, but it is a single sentence. By breaking it up, the author carefully controls both the rhythm and the pacing. The alliteration, sensory details, and repetition create a mood of magic and mystery that hooks readers. It makes them want to turn the page and keep reading. This is the kind of craftsmanship that makes Fleming one of our favorite nonfiction authors.

ACTIVITY 7.1

Exploring Voice in Nonfiction

After reading aloud a few pages of *Pink Is for Blobfish: Discovering the World's Perfectly Pink Animals* by Jess Keating, invite a few student volunteers to describe the book's voice. They might choose words like "lively," "playful," or "humorous." They also might notice that it seems like the author is speaking directly to them.

Next, read aloud a few pages of *A Butterfly Is Patient* by Dianna Hutts Aston. Divide the class into small groups and encourage the teams to compare the voices of the two books. They should notice that *A Butterfly Is Patient* features a more wondrous, lyrical voice.

Using a document camera, project the "Pretty in Pink!" sidebar on page 3 of *Pink Is for Blobfish: Discovering the World's Perfectly Pink Animals* on your classroom interactive whiteboard. After giving students time to turn and talk about the author's sentence lengths, word choices, and punctuation decisions, record their ideas about how these elements affect the voice of the passage. Did they notice the alliteration in the first line or the exclamation point at the end? What do they notice about the wording of the last sentence?

Now project the smaller, secondary text on page 3 of *A Butterfly Is Patient* on your classroom interactive whiteboard and listen in as your students analyze how the author crafted the voice. If students struggle with this task, ask the following questions to guide their thinking:

- Does it seem like the author is talking directly to readers?
- Is Aston creating an image in the reader's mind?
- How are the sentence structure and punctuation of this passage different from the "Pretty in Pink!" sidebar?

Finally, divide the class into small groups, and invite each team to create a Venn diagram that lists text characteristics of a lively voice versus a lyrical voice. Allow time for the teams to share their Venn diagrams with the rest of the class.

Language Matters

From alliteration to zeugma, there are dozens of different kinds of language devices, and all of them can enrich nonfiction writing. As authors craft their prose, they carefully select each and every word, so that they can create text bursting with the kind of rich, powerful language that engages young audiences (Siu-Ruyan 1998).

When used skillfully, figurative language infuses writing with combinations of sounds and syllables that are especially pleasing to the human ear. As a result, these language devices can infuse a piece of nonfiction writing with a strong lyrical voice. Consider this lovely passage from *We Are Grateful: Otsaliheliga* by Traci Sorell:

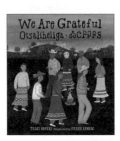

When cool breezes blow and leaves fall,
we say otsaliheliga . . .
. . . as shell shakers dance all night around the fire,
burnt cedar's scent drifts upward during the
Great New Moon Ceremony.

Notice how the author makes excellent use of alliteration, sensory details, and imagery to transport young readers to the Cherokee Nation's autumn Great New Moon Ceremony and show them how special it is.

In *Frog Song*, author Brenda Z. Guiberson skillfully employs a combination of vibrant verbs, similes, alliteration, repetition, and onomatopoeia to enliven her text and highlight the incredible diversity of frogs and their mating calls. Here's a brief excerpt.

In Spain, the song of the male midwife toad clangs like a bell. **TINK TINK TINK TINK!** He carries a string of sticky eggs and crouches under a wet log to keep them moist. **SQUIZZLE-SQUIZ.** When he feels the tadpoles squirming, he hops, hops, hops to find a pool where they can hatch.

During the revision process, Guiberson sometimes uses a thesaurus to help her find the perfect word. She also reads her work aloud, listening to every syllable and sound, and asks other people to read it to her. "I pay close attention," she says. "Where do they hesitate or stumble? Where does the writing seem flat or quiet? What could be stronger? I go through this process several times."

Combining language devices like puns, rhyme, alliteration, and surprising phrasing can make writing more humorous and playful, which is perfect for authors interested in crafting a lively voice. Consider these amusing headings from *Poison: Deadly Deeds, Perilous Professions, and Murderous Medicines* by Sarah Albee:

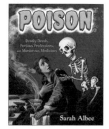

Toxic Plots, Poison Pots, and Shipboard Shots
I Came, I Saw, I Poisoned
Heir Today, Gone Tomorrow
Finger-licking Bad

Albee includes this kind of language to help middle-grade readers see just how "amazing and exciting and interesting history actually is."

Albee notes that while her early drafts often include some lively writing, enriching her prose with "humor and energy is something I usually do at a late stage of revision. I carefully examine each sentence and think: How can I make this funnier, or more vivid, for my reader?"

To get her creative juices flowing, Albee often makes lists of words that relate to her topic. Then she tries to think of alliterative adjectives, rhymes, and synonyms that might be pertinent. She also looks for ways to turn clichés or familiar phrases on their heads, such as I Came, I Saw, I Poisoned and Heir Today, Gone Tomorrow. "It can take a lot of mental energy to come up with a good turn of phrase," says Albee, "but it's so satisfying when I do!"

ACTIVITY 7.2

Appreciating Rich Language in Nonfiction

The best way for students to get a feel for the flow of rich, engaging language is to analyze finely crafted expository literature and narrative nonfiction books. Invite students to choose one of the eight titles below and type or write out a few pages by hand, so the text looks similar to the drafts they write, and they can evaluate it in the same way that they analyze their own writing.

Before She Was Harriet: The Story of Harriet Tubman by Lesa Cline-Ransome

Frog Song by Brenda Z. Guiberson

Giant Squid by Candace Fleming

If You Find a Rock by Peggy Christian

If You Hopped Like a Frog by David M. Schwartz

Planting the Wild Garden by Kathryn O. Galbraith

Squirrels Leap, Squirrels Sleep by April Pulley Sayre

We Are Grateful: Otsaliheliga by Traci Sorell

After organizing the class into small groups based on the books they selected, encourage the teams to identify key language features and highlight them with different colors. Students who type the text can use colored text in the computer file, and students who write the text by hand can use colored pencils or highlighting markers. The following color code works well for the titles listed above:

red = vivid verbs

blue = similes, metaphors, and other comparisons

green = alliteration

purple = repetition

orange = onomatopoeia

An eighth grader has identified and highlighted the vivid verbs (red), comparisons (blue), alliteration (green), and even one example of onomatopoeia (orange) in one of her rough drafts. Now she's adding more rich language to the piece!

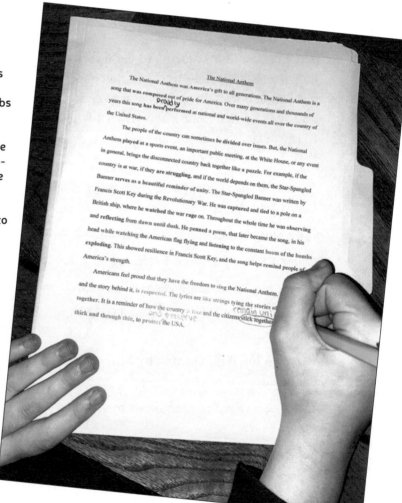

After students complete this task, invite them to highlight these same language features in one of their rough drafts. Can they find spots where replacing a verb or adding a comparison or language device could strengthen their writing? As students complete this task, encourage them to share their changes with a classmate.

What's Your Point of View?

In the past, nearly all nonfiction books for children featured third-person point of view, and many still do. But more and more, authors of expository literature and narrative nonfiction are experimenting with other kinds of narration.

Second-Person Narration

As you read the following excerpt from *Tiny Creatures: The World of Microbes* by Nicola Davies, notice how addressing readers with "you" makes the information relevant to their lives and their world:

> Right now there are more microbes living on your skin than there are people on Earth, and there are ten or even a hundred times as many as that in your stomach.

Now take a look at a few lines from *Bone by Bone: Comparing Animal Skeletons* by Sara Levine:

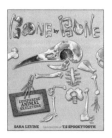

> Can you imagine how you'd look if we added some bones to your spine?
>
> What if your vertebrae didn't stop at your rear end?
>
> What if they kept going?
>
> YOU'D HAVE A TAIL!

Tails are made of vertebrae. Lots of animals have tails.
They wag on happy dogs and sweep side to side to help
alligators swim through the water.

According to Levine, as she crafted her manuscript, she looked for
ways to "make learning interactive, relevant, and fun." She thought
about how "children enjoy being addressed directly and being active
participants in responding to questions that make them think, especially
about silly possibilities."

As you can see in this excerpt from *Flying Deep: Climb Inside
Deep-Sea Submersible ALVIN* by Michelle Cusolito, second-
person point of view can also be used to take young readers on an
armchair journey to places few people will ever go.

Imagine
you're a pilot
of *Alvin*,
a deep-sea submersible
barely big enough for three . . .

Lower yourself
through *Alvin*'s hatch.
Flip on oxygen—
pssssssssssss.
Switch on carbon dioxide scrubber—
zzzzzzzzhhhhhhhh.

Isn't it amazing how Cusolito's use of sensory details and second-
person narration puts readers right in the middle of the action? What
a powerful way to engage and connect with children!

First-Person Narration

When you think of nonfiction with a first-person point of view,
autobiographical accounts like *Brown Girl Dreaming* by Jacqueline
Woodson, *Hey, Kiddo* by Jarrett Krosoczka, or *The Scraps Book:
Notes from a Colorful Life* by Lois Ehlert probably come to mind.
But authors are also trying some exciting new things.

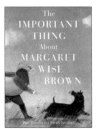

For example, *The Important Thing About Margaret Wise Brown* by Mac Barnett is a picture book biography written in the form of a personal essay, resulting in a book that's as much about Barnett's view of the world as it is about a legendary children's book author.

Similarly, *Something Rotten: A Fresh Look at Roadkill* by Heather L. Montgomery takes an astonishingly innovative approach to a topic that might turn some stomachs. First-person narration allows the author's fascination—and hesitation—to come through loud and clear. Here's how Montgomery describes her feelings as she was researching the book.

> Every time I passed a carcass on the road, things inside my body wrenched. My heart screamed at the injustice, but my mind marveled at the bobcat's body. My eyes teared with sadness while my fingers begged to touch that velvet fur.
>
> I couldn't stop myself from parking and looking, from asking and wondering. I felt like a voyeur but my feet kept inching closer, closer to the dead bodies. Then one day I gave in to inquiry.

We love how Montgomery's description is so human, so normal, so universal, and yet something that few people would dare to admit. We look forward to seeing more creative experimentation like this in the future of children's books.

That's Not Nonfiction!

In fiction, first-person narration is powerful because it allows readers to see the world from the main character's perspective. In recent years, some authors have tried to bring this same kind of intimacy and engagement to our understanding of historic figures by writing biographies in first person.

In books like *I Am Rosa Parks* by Brad Meltzer and *Solving the Puzzle Under the Sea: Marie Tharp Maps the Ocean Floor* by Robert Burleigh, iconic figures from the past seem to tell their own stories. But in fact, the authors aren't quoting their subjects. They're inventing the text by putting words in the mouths of their subjects. And that makes these books informational fiction—not nonfiction.

As we mentioned in Chapter 1, informational fiction is based on documented facts but takes creative liberties, such as made-up dialogue or imagined scenes, in an effort to make the book more engaging. Informational fiction also includes "pseudo-narratives"—fact-based books that have an expository writing style but resemble a narrative because the information is reported by a fictional narrator, such as an animal or inanimate object or a person other than the author (Englert and Hibert 1984). Examples include the following:

Beavers: The Superpower Field Guide by Rachel Poliquin

The Deadliest Creature in the World by Brenda Z. Guiberson

Hey, Water by Antoinette Portis

I, Fly: The Buzz About Flies and How Awesome They Are by Bridget Heos

One Proud Penny by Randy Siegel

Sun: One in a Billion by Stacey McAnulty

In some cases, these books can be a fun and effective way to share ideas and information with young readers, but they should **not** take the place of nonfiction books in your classroom or library collection. It's critically important that students develop the skills necessary to recognize what's real, what's true, what's verifiable, and what's not.

ACTIVITY 7.3

Exploring Point of View in Nonfiction

Read aloud portions of *Birds of a Feather: Bowerbirds and Me* by Susan L. Roth (first-person narration), *Flying Deep: Climb Inside Deep-Sea Submersible ALVIN* by Michelle Cusolito (second-person narration), and *Stretch to the Sun: From a Tiny Sprout to the Tallest Tree on Earth* by Carrie A. Pearson (third-person narration) and work with students to iden-

tify each book's point of view. When the class seems to have a good understanding of the three kinds of narration, organize students into small groups. Give each team a packet of sticky notes and two or three nonfiction books (some expository literature, some narrative nonfiction) with different points of view. Some possibilities include the following:

Dinosaurs by the Numbers by Steve Jenkins

If You Decide to Go to the Moon by Faith McNulty

If You Hopped Like a Frog by David M. Schwartz

Poet: The Remarkable Story of George Moses Horton by Don Tate

The Scraps Book: Notes from a Colorful Life by Lois Ehlert

This Is How We Do It: One Day in the Lives of Seven Kids from Around the World by Matt LaMothe

Then invite students to classify the books by point of view and label each one with a sticky note.

After reading *Poet: The Remarkable Story of George Moses Horton* by Don Tate, these fourth graders added a sticky note indicating that the book has a third-person point of view.

When the teams complete this task, encourage each group to rotate to a different station, leaving their books behind. Students should review the books at their new station and discuss how the previous group classified the books. If they disagree with the previous group, they should add a second sticky note explaining their rationale.

Repeat this process until each group has reviewed all the books. Then have a brief class discussion about books that have multiple sticky notes on them.

Experimenting with Voice and Point of View

After reviewing the definitions of *voice*, *first-person point of view*, and *third-person point of view* with students, use a document camera to display Table 7.1 on page 114 on your classroom interactive white-board. As you read through the text, discuss how the writing in each column is different, and examine the craft moves utilized to vary the voice and point of view. (At this point in the lesson, do not point out to students that the writing samples in the third column—first-person from spider's perspective—are informational fiction.)

Next, let the class know that they're going to write similar pieces about an animal they observe. Ideally, you'll be able to take the class outdoors where they can find a bird, spider, insect, or other small animal in its natural habitat. Another possibility is encouraging students to take turns observing a class pet. If your students aren't able to observe a live animal, divide the class into small groups and invite each team to view a webcam or watch video clips that show an animal in its natural environment. (Look for suitable material online or in the school library. You may also want to ask your school librarian for assistance.) After watching an animal of their choice closely for several minutes, the children should sketch the creature and carefully record everything they notice in their notebook.

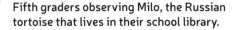

Fifth graders observing Milo, the Russian tortoise that lives in their school library.

TABLE 7.1: Varying Voice and Point of View

	First-Person Point of View; Excited, Wondrous Voice	Third-Person Point of View; Serious, Scientific Voice	First-Person from Spider's Perspective
	Wow! Look at this fabulous female *Argiope* spider. I'd recognize this spectacular species anywhere, anytime. Her size and colorful body and legs are a dead giveaway.	Slightly blurred image of female *Argiope* spider perched on her web. Note the second leg touching the web, allowing her to detect even the slightest vibration.	I'm really enjoying stretching out in the sun this morning. It's been such a rainy week. I can finally build a web and try to catch a little bit of grub.
	Oh no, I accidentally shook the web! Now the spider is nervous. See how her legs are coiled in?	After disturbing the web, the spider has curled her legs to stay balanced. Note the pattern of the web's threads visible at the bottom of the image.	Yikes! That shaking was caused by something a whole lot bigger than a bug! I'm gonna coil up tight and wait it out. I don't want to abandon my web if I don't have to.
	Finally, the spider had enough of me. As she scurried away, I ended up with a nice photo of her abdomen.	Excellent view of the abdomen as the spider seeks safety on one of the branches anchoring her web.	"Oh no! I see a giant's shadow. I better run for cover. Whatever's out there must be pretty dangerous!"

When everyone has completed their observations, give your class time to use words and pictures to create three short pieces about their animal—one written in first person with an excited, wondrous voice; one written in third person with a serious, scientific voice; and one written in first person from the animal's point of view.

When the students seem ready, invite a few volunteers to share their pieces with the rest of the class. Then ask the teams to consider the following question: *Are the pieces we've created fiction or nonfiction?* They should be ready to defend their answer.

Two fifth-grade writing samples created by students after observing Milo

1. I can't believe how fast Milo is. I can't believe how this Russian tortoise is rushin' around so fast.

2. The tortoise takes his head into his shell when he feels uncomfortable. It is also a defense mechanism. He also has 4 sharp claws that gives him traction.

3. Look at all these beings. This lady takes me out of my habitat and then she won't let me explore. The nerve! I am officially on strike! I will not eat until they leave.

#2: Milo keeps tucking his head into his shell when ever we try to steer him back into the center of the mats. Milo has four sharp claws that help him have traction on the mats. Milo's shell is a greenish-brown. His legs, tail and face are more of a dark brown.

#3: Aaahh! so many people! There seems to be danger nearby, I better run as fast as possible, but everywhere I look theres another person! I wish I had more space to explore! Geez, what do they want from me? What does a Tortoise have to do to get some space around here? Stop shoving lettuce in my face! I'm not going to eat! That lady keeps picking me up and turning me around! But I do have to admit, they're pretty interesting!

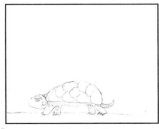

#1: Cool! I can't believe how fast Milo the Russian Tortoise is! He seems a little bit uncomfortable in his new environment. He won't eat the lettuce yet. He keeps going to the edge of the mats, we have to put him back into the center the mats. Every time I try to stop him from going off the mat, he just keeps pushing against my hand. I can also feel his breath sometimes.

To bring the activity to a close, read a few passages from the informational fiction titles *The Deadliest Creature in the World* by Brenda Z. Guiberson and *Sun: One in a Billion* by Stacey McAnulty. Then ask your class: *Are these books fiction or nonfiction? Explain your rationale.*

As students share their ideas, the rest of the class should feel free to agree or respectfully disagree. They may also ask questions and offer their own insights.

Now that you're armed with strategies and activities for helping students study nonfiction craft moves with expository literature and narrative nonfiction, Chapter 8 will help you take the next step. It's bursting with fun, practical ideas for introducing, celebrating, and evaluating all 5 Kinds of Nonfiction with students.

"I like that nonfiction books really make you think about things for a while and then sometimes your thinking changes."

—Ryan, fifth grader

Introducing Nonfiction Books

From the moment students enter the classroom on their first day of school, they should be steeped in an environment that respects and honors nonfiction and fiction equally. One of the easiest ways to send this message is with prominent, well-lit displays of colorful, enticing fiction, narrative nonfiction, and expository nonfiction books. As the year progresses, you can continue to show your enthusiasm for a wide range of books with book talks, preview stacks, and book tastings. These kinds of activities are the perfect way to share and spread nonfiction joy.

Book Displays

In many classrooms, nonfiction is relegated to a few battered tubs labeled by topic, and teachers share these books only during relevant social studies and science units. We'd like to encourage educators to rethink the way they select, engage with, and utilize nonfiction children's books. Students should have opportunities to interact with all 5 Kinds of Nonfiction every single day.

When nonfiction is reserved for content-area lessons, students notice. They get the idea that these books aren't meant for or worthy of everyday use. But the truth is that nonfiction can be enticing *and* educational, interesting *and* informative. Students need to know that any and all nonfiction is a valid and valuable choice for independent reading (Stead 2014). That's why every classroom and every school library should include a wide range of finely crafted nonfiction titles about sharks and gymnastics and pyramids and robots and a host of other topics that students can't resist.

As Stephanie Harvey and Annie Ward (2017) say in their book *From Striving to Thriving: How to Grow Confident, Capable Readers*, "Build a library for the readers you expect; customize it for the readers you meet."

But making the books available isn't enough. Educators have to draw attention to them. And one of the best ways to do that is with rotating book displays. During the first week of school, feature a mix of fiction and nonfiction books about starting school and ways children around the world travel to school. Here are some suggested titles.

The Day You Begin by Jacqueline Woodson (fiction)

First Day Jitters by Julie Danneberg (fiction)

If I Built a School by Chris Van Dusen (fiction)

One World, One Day by Barbara Kerley (nonfiction)

School's First Day of School by Adam Rex (fiction)

This Is How We Do It: One Day in the Lives of Seven Kids from Around the World by Matt LaMothe (nonfiction)

Throughout the week, read the books aloud. Discuss what they have in common and how they're different. Remember, an expository book like *This Is How We Do It: One Day in the Lives of Seven Kids from Around the World* doesn't have to be read cover to cover. You can just read a few double-page spreads.

During Week 2, feature expository nonfiction from all four categories—active, browseable, traditional, and expository literature. For Week 3, display fiction titles. And during Week 4, feature narrative nonfiction. If you repeat this pattern a few times, students will begin to get a sense of all the different kinds of books available to them. They will also get the message that you value ALL types of books equally.

As the year progresses, choose one week to display a range of browseable nonfiction. Another week, you can feature just active nonfiction or just expository literature. You can also select text sets that are related to a holiday, current event, or your science or social studies unit. Include both nonfiction and fiction titles to appeal to a broad range of students. Because no classroom collection can possibly serve all these needs, consider borrowing books from other teachers, the school library, and the public library.

Creating Nonfiction Book Displays

This team of fifth graders created a text set that features STEM-themed nonfiction books with strong verbs.

During the second half of the year, allow students to form teams and create their own text sets for display. The books in the text set must have something in common—a theme or concept, a text structure, a writing style, the voice (lively or lyrical), and so on. Encourage students to be creative in their choices, and then summarize their thinking on an index card. The teams may enjoy asking the rest of the class to guess what the books in their text set have in common.

Book Talks

How often do you read a book because it's recommended by someone you know and trust? Students are no different. That's why book talks are a great way to get students excited about books and reading. Like book displays, these two- to four-minute oral advertisements can make students aware of the wide range of books available in your classroom collection (Eurich 2011).

Chances are you've done book talks to share your passion for fiction books, but have you ever tried this technique with nonfiction titles? We'd like to challenge you to booktalk at least one book from each category in the 5 Kinds of Nonfiction over a five-week period. So that your enthusiasm is genuine, choose active nonfiction books related to one of your hobbies or a skill you'd like to learn. Select browseable books, traditional books, and expository literature about topics that really do make you curious, and find narrative nonfiction titles about people you truly admire. Don't be afraid to choose books that are below grade level, especially if you think your

striving readers might enjoy them (Harvey and Ward 2017).

When Marlene was a classroom teacher, one of her favorite times to do book talks was when the Scholastic book order arrived. It was a great way to get students excited about the new titles she had purchased with book club points. Book talks also work well during snack, right after recess, or when you have a few extra minutes before art or P.E.

When you booktalk nonfiction, start with a "hook" that will capture your students' interest. Then share a few fascinating facts or irresistible details. You may want to read a short excerpt or show a visual that will engage

Sample Book Talk

Imagine you woke up one morning and had jackrabbit ears! What would you look like? Would the world sound different?

In the expository nonfiction picture book *What If You Had Animal Ears*, author Sandra Markle introduces us to eleven animals with amazing ears. Did you know a jackrabbit's ears give off body heat to help it stay cool? And a Tasmanian devil's ears blush red when it's excited or upset? There's so much interesting information in this book, and it's chock-full of illustrations that will make you laugh out loud! At the end of the book, you'll find out what makes **your** ears so special.

young readers. When you're done, be sure to display the book so students can take a look at it later. If you give a book your blessing, chances are students will want to read it (Gambrell 1996; Miller and Kelley 2014).

ACTIVITY 8.2

Student Book Talks

As the year progresses, invite students to develop their own nonfiction book talks about books they love. To help them, we have included two Planning a Book Talk tipsheets (one for grades 2–3, and one for grades 4–8) in Appendix D.

As students listen to book talks given by you or their classmates, encourage them to keep track of titles that sound interesting by creating a "to-be-read" list on the last page of their reader's notebook.

Preview Stacks

As we discussed in Chapter 4, allowing students to choose the books they read increases their motivation as well as their comprehension (Guthrie et al. 2007), but some students struggle to find books they're passionate about. And just about anyone can get stuck in a reading rut from time to time. That's when preview stacks can come in handy.

A preview stack is a collection of books that you curate for a particular student with their interests and reading level in mind (Miller 2009). Not only can these customized stacks jump-start your students' reading lives, they can also help you understand your students' fiction and nonfiction reading preferences in a deeper way (Harvey and Ward 2017). For example, you could build preview stacks with one book from each of the 5 Kinds of Nonfiction and sit with students as they explore and discuss the books. Make notes about which ones intrigue the students most, and use that information to plan instruction and make decisions about what books to add to the classroom collection.

Whenever you notice a student struggling to find a book or stay focused during independent reading time, build a stack of books for them. You can include titles from your classroom book collection as well as the school library. As you hand the preview stack to the student say something like, "I know you like books about the environment, and I remember your favorite categories are browseable and expository literature. I found these titles just for you."

This simple act will make a deep and lasting impression on the child. It will show them that you understand and honor their unique interests and that you care about their development as a reader.

Book Tastings

To expose students in grades 2–8 to a broad "menu" of fiction and nonfiction books, decorate your classroom like a restaurant and make stacks of books representing various fiction genres (mystery, science fiction, realistic fiction, historical fiction, etc.) and the 5 Kinds of Nonfiction. Use the Category Feature Cards found in Appendix D to

Fourth graders will sample a menu of fiction and 5 Kinds of Nonfiction at an inviting classroom book tasting. As students enter, they will receive a name card and a table assignment.

create signs for the nonfiction stacks. Then design similar labels for the fiction genres. When each stack has a sign, place the piles on tables around the classroom.

As students enter the room, divide them into small groups and invite the teams to rotate from table to table, reading each book's title and first two pages. They should also skim through the entire book and look at the visuals. Encourage the children to make a list of books they'd like to "sample" later. Serving snacks (if permissible) as students move around the room can make this activity more fun.

Working with your school librarian and the children's librarian from your community's public library, you could plan a Family Literacy Night with book-tasting stations in the school gym or cafeteria. You could also host the event in the community room of your local library.

As families arrive, encourage them to explore and discuss a broad range of books. It's the perfect opportunity to show parents that all books are valuable and that they should respect and encourage their children's independent reading choices. Families may even discover nonfiction books that can make great bedtime read-alouds.

At the end of the evening, encourage families to borrow some of the books they found most intriguing. If the children don't have a public library card, this is the perfect time for them to get one!

Celebrating Nonfiction Books

Once students are aware of the many different kinds of nonfiction available to them, it's time to explore and celebrate these titles. You can do this through read-alouds and book clubs. We also recommend a wonderful whole-school event called March Madness Nonfiction.

Read-Alouds

We'd like to start this section with a shout-out to our friends at #class roombookaday. We wrote this section with their comments, questions, and suggestions in mind.

If you haven't heard of #classroombookaday, it's a great strategy for incorporating a rich assortment of read-alouds into your classroom routine. Developed by Wisconsin school librarian Jillian Heise (www .heisereads.com), it involves taking ten to fifteen minutes a day to read aloud and briefly discuss a fiction or nonfiction picture book. What makes it special is Jillian's clever idea of displaying the book covers on a wall or bulletin board, so it's easy to refer back to them later in the year. For example, students can make thematic connections between titles. They can also compare craft moves employed by authors and artistic techniques employed by the illustrators.

A #classroombookaday chart inspires students throughout the year.

To learn more about #classroombookaday and join the growing #classroombookaday community, you can join the vibrant Facebook group (www.facebook.com/groups/classroombookaday/) where educators discuss logistics and make book recommendations.

One of the reasons #classroombookaday is becoming so popular is because teachers and students treasure read-aloud time AND an extensive body of research shows that this practice has a powerful positive effect on student engagement, thinking, and reading achievement (Layne 2015).

That's the good news. The bad news is that nonfiction read-alouds are rare (Stead 2014; Vardell 1998; Yopp and Yopp 2006). We'd like to change that because, as you learned in Chapter 3, many students prefer expository texts. Since 42 percent of students prefer expository nonfiction (Repaskey, Schumm, and Johnson 2017) and students choose nonfiction for pleasure reading about 40 percent of the time (Doiron 2003), we'd like to encourage educators to select nonfiction books as read-alouds about 40 percent of the time. If you're doing #classroombookaday, that means choosing a nonfiction title—preferably an expository nonfiction title—twice a week.

This goal may sound good in theory, but we've found that many educators are hesitant to read nonfiction aloud. We hear the same three questions over and over.

- How do I locate appropriate nonfiction titles?

- How do I read nonfiction aloud in a way that engages students?

- How do I encourage and facilitate student responses to a nonfiction read-aloud?

Luckily, we have some advice that should help.

Locating Appropriate Books

In Appendix B, you'll find a section called Resources for Finding High-Quality Nonfiction. It includes a list of highly regarded nonfiction awards as well as two blogs that we admire. These are good places to find finely crafted narrative and expository nonfiction. However, not all of these titles will work well as read-alouds, so Appendix E provides a list of thirty-six picture books that are perfect for sharing in ten minutes or less.

As you search for more books on your own in the future, it's important to think about how students will respond. Look for books that will engage young listeners right away. For example, *An Egg Is Quiet* and *Trout Are Made of Trees* have provocative titles that will immediately spark curiosity.

Read the beginnings of books to see if they have language or concepts that will hook your audience and make students want to hear more. For example, here's the first line of *Birds of a Feather: Bowerbirds and Me* by Susan L. Roth:

The differences between a bowerbird and me are fewer than you might expect.

And here's how *Pipsqueaks, Slowpokes, and Stinkers: Celebrating Animal Underdogs* by Melissa Stewart begins:

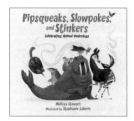

Everyone loves elephants. They're so big and strong.

Everyone respects cheetahs. They're so fast and fierce.

But this book isn't about animals we admire. It's about the unsung underdogs of the animal world. Don't you think it's time someone paid attention to them?

Who could possibly resist openings like these?

As you preview potential books, look for titles that aren't loaded with academic vocabulary. If more than 10 percent of the words are unfamiliar to your students, it's probably not a good choice for reading aloud (Stead 2014).

Reading Nonfiction Aloud: Tips and Tricks

Reading nonfiction picture books aloud can be tricky because they often contain significantly more words than fiction picture books. And even if the art is enticing and the writing is engaging and the information is fascinating, a picture book read-aloud shouldn't last more than ten minutes. As we plan a nonfiction read-aloud, we ask ourselves some important questions.

- What parts of the book should we highlight?

- Should we skip over anything?

- Would additional visuals or props improve the audience's experience?

- Would using a document camera help?

Sometimes we make the right decisions on the first try. But other times, the kids surprise us, and we make adjustments as we go along.

In a book like *Flying Frogs and Walking Fish: Leaping Lemurs, Tumbling Toads, Jet-Propelled Jellyfish, and More Surprising Ways That Animals Move* by Steve Jenkins and Robin Page, some double-page spreads have six animal examples. Depending on the age of your audience, that may be too much. It's fine to let a student volunteer choose just one example for you to share with the class. Then, if children want to know more, they can read the rest of the examples themselves later.

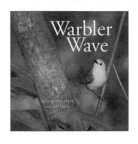

In a book like *Cute as an Axolotl: Discovering the World's Most Adorable Animals* by Jess Keating, which has a lot of information on each page, you can share just a couple of spreads as a read-aloud. As with *Flying Frogs and Walking Fish*, you can encourage interested students to read the rest of the book on their own.

Books like *Warbler Wave* by April Pulley Sayre have a short, poetic main text with lots of interesting extra information in the back matter. Feel free to take your time savoring the gorgeous main text and the stunning photographs with students. Then, as time permits, share just a few sections of the back matter. When it comes to nonfiction read-alouds, there's no rule that says you have to read every single word!

During the read-aloud, be sure to put expression into your reading. Be animated. Be dramatic. Show that you're eager to discover whatever fascinating facts and amazing ideas the author will reveal.

Encouraging Student Responses

Please believe us when we say that encouraging students to respond to nonfiction read-alouds is the last thing you need to worry about.

When you read fiction aloud, students don't know what to expect. The story could go in any direction at all. The only limit is the author's imagination. As a result, during fiction read-alouds, students often patiently wait to hear how the story will unfold.

But students come to nonfiction read-alouds armed with a powerful

tool—their prior knowledge. They'll have a cornucopia of ideas and opinions before you even open the book. In fact, one of your students may even be a mini-expert on the topic. Instead of passively waiting to hear the story, children will be eager to contribute (Stead 2014). All you have to do is let them. Encourage children to talk with one another about what they're hearing and thinking and wondering. Every once in a while, stop reading and invite students to share their thoughts and questions.

Although organic student-led conversations are often sufficient, in some cases, you may want to document a nonfiction read-aloud experience. In his wonderful article "Nurturing the Inquiring Mind Through the Nonfiction Read-Aloud," Tony Stead (2014) suggests recording student thinking before, during, and after the read-aloud using a table with the following headings: "What We Think We Know," "Confirmed," "We Don't Think This Anymore," "Exciting New Information," "Wonderings." This strategy works especially well when students come to the read-aloud with misconceptions about a topic. It can also spark inquiry and guide students as they independently research and write about a topic.

Book Clubs

If you belong to a book club, you know that half the fun is socializing with your friends. The same is true for a student book club. Besides encouraging students to talk about reading, which enhances their comprehension, book clubs give students an opportunity to practice life skills like taking turns, expressing opinions, listening to others, and working collaboratively. When students read and explore nonfiction in this way, they're more likely to develop the ability to recognize when they don't understand the text and employ such problem-solving strategies as skipping ahead, rereading, asking questions, using a dictionary, and reading the passage aloud (Mazzoni and Gambrell 1996; Zimmerman and Hutchins 2003).

Teachers often think of fiction first for student book clubs, but don't underestimate the power of book clubs with a nonfiction focus. Try introducing nonfiction titles that represent all 5 Kinds of Nonfiction and cover a broad range of topics. After a brief book talk, ask students to select their first and second choices, and then entice them to join the club with these titles.

During club time, students review their book, decide how many pages they'll read each day or week, and then go off and read on their own. They meet regularly for peer-led discussions of the book in parts and, eventually, as a whole.

These fourth graders are participating in a Strong Women book club. The girls on the left are comparing two picture book biographies written by Lesa Cline-Ransome. The girls on the right are discussing a biography collection by Chelsea Clinton.

TEACHING **TIP**

Initially, you can suggest books for club members to read, but as the students become more confident readers and begin to develop their own opinions about nonfiction books, encourage them to select their own titles, just as adult book club members would. We recommend that students read reviews in *School Library Journal, Booklist,* or *Kirkus Reviews* to discover new nonfiction titles. Your school or community librarian probably subscribes to these publications and can share past issues with you.

Students are motivated by the idea of participating in an "adult" activity. They quickly take ownership of the club and, after some modeling, are able to engage in meaningful conversations about the books. The key to helping the striving readers is having books they can access, or putting supports in place, such as audio books, to assist students when they need it.

In *Igniting a Passion for Reading*, Steven Layne (2009) recommends what he calls First Read Clubs. When a teacher or librarian gets new books, student volunteers preview them and select one to read. They then report back to the teacher, librarian, or class, sharing a little bit about the book, how they would classify it, and who they think might enjoy it. The books can then be marked with labels that say, "This book was first read by _____."

March Madness Nonfiction

Inspired by the annual March Madness basketball tournament, literacy coach Shelley Moody and instructional coach Valerie Glueck at Williams Elementary School in Oakland, Maine, developed a monthlong, whole-school activity in which students read sixteen nonfiction picture books (some narrative, some expository literature) and select their favorite.

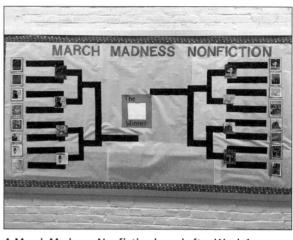

A March Madness Nonfiction board after Week 1

During Week 1, half the classes read the eight books on the right-hand side of the board, and the other half of the school reads the eight books on the left-hand side of the board. Classrooms discuss the content and structure of the books as well as their favorite features. Then students vote on pairs of books to determine which titles will move on to the Elite Eight.

During Week 2, each class reads the four winning books on the opposite side of the board. Then students participate in rich classroom discussions and vote to select the Final Four.

During Week 3, classes spend time reviewing the four finalists and then vote for the March Madness Nonfiction Champion.

During the final week, students gather for a whole-school assembly. Following a parade of books that includes one child from each classroom, the winning book is announced. And the crowd goes wild!

According to Shelley, "The goal of this event is to inspire curiosity, to build background knowledge, and to put outstanding nonfiction books in the hands of our students. It's hard to capture in words the energy and excitement about books that March Madness has created in our school community." And Valerie says, "March Madness is a springboard for discussions of text features and structures, vocabulary, and author's purpose" (Stewart 2020).

Adapting March Madness Nonfiction

After reading about the incredible success of Williams Elementary School's March Madness Nonfiction program, Pike Elementary School in Andover, Massachusetts, decided to host a similar event at their school to build enthusiasm for an author visit with Melissa Stewart. They selected sixteen of her books and, over a one-month period, followed the process the staff at Williams School had developed. The winning book was announced on the day of Melissa's visit.

Even if an author visit isn't a possibility for your school, an author study like this one can build excitement for nonfiction reading and give students an opportunity to look closely at the writing style and craft moves of one author. Mary Kay Carson, Kelly Milner Halls, Steve Jenkins, Sandra Markle, April Pulley Sayre, and Sally M. Walker would all be good choices for this kind of activity.

Evaluating Nonfiction Books

Once students have experience exploring and discussing nonfiction content and craft, they're ready to delve deeper. The following activities encourage children to think critically and evaluate the nonfiction books they're reading.

ACTIVITY 8.3

Nonfiction Smackdown! Evaluating and Comparing Two Books

In this activity, which was developed by Judi Paradis, a teacher-librarian at Plympton Elementary School in Waltham, Massachusetts, students read two nonfiction books on the same topic. They can be two narrative titles, two expository titles, or one of each.

Students evaluate, classify, and compare the titles from any of the 5 Kinds of Nonfiction, and then document their thinking on the Nonfiction Smackdown! recording sheet found in Appendix D on page 155. These worksheets can be hung around the room or placed in a folder, so that classmates can use the information to help them select books in the future.

Here are some sample pairings.

Death Eaters: Meet Nature's Scavengers by Kelly Milner Halls and *Rotten! Vultures, Beetles, Slime and Nature's Other Decomposers* by Anita Sanchez

Dog Days of History: The Incredible Story of Our Best Friends by Sarah Albee and *Made for Each Other: Why Dogs and People Are Perfect Partners* by Dorothy Hinshaw Patent

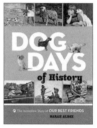 

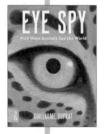 

Eye Spy: Wild Ways Animals See the World by Guillaume Duprat and *What If You Had Animal Eyes?* by Sandra Markle

Flying Deep: Climb Inside Deep-Sea Submersible ALVIN by Michelle Cusolito and *Otis and Will Discover the Deep: The Record-Setting Dive of the Bathysphere* by Barb Rosenstock

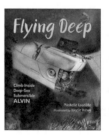 

A Seed Is the Start by Melissa Stewart and *Seeds Move* by Robin Page

Sibert Smackdown! Selecting an Award Winner

The Sibert Smackdown is an activity intended to build enthusiasm for the Robert F. Sibert Informational Book Medal, which is given each year as part of the American Library Association's annual Youth Media Awards. Although the winning books can be picture books or middle-grade long-form titles, the Sibert Smackdown! focuses on picture books because their length makes them more manageable to read and evaluate in a school setting.

A fourth grader getting ready to defend his Sibert Smackdown choice to his classmates

To participate in this activity, students read the ten nonfiction picture books on your class's Mock Sibert list. You can select the books (some narrative, some expository literature) yourself or use the list that Melissa posts on her blog (celebratescience.blogspot.com) each year. Melissa's list includes titles that have strong kid appeal, will promote good discussions, and can be used as mentor texts to reinforce the research techniques and craft moves included in most state ELA standards.

After reading the Mock titles, students choose their two favorites and complete the Sibert Smackdown! recording sheet located in Appendix D on page 156. This recording sheet, which features a kid-friendly version of the criteria considered by the real Sibert committee, helps students to evaluate, classify, and compare books before they vote for a winner.

Student votes can be compiled to determine individual classroom winners as well as a single whole-school winner. In some schools, students watch the livestream of the ALA Youth Media Award announcements to see which nonfiction books were selected by the Sibert committee. Just imagine the excitement when a school's winner really does receive the Sibert Medal or a Sibert Honor!

Participating schools can use the Twitter hashtag #SibertSmackdown to share the experience with one another, to swap ideas for additional related activities, and to discuss and compare the titles they chose as winners. At some schools, students record their rationale for choosing a particular book using Padlet, Flipgrid, or posters. One school developed voting forms that allow students to use words and pictures to explain their choices. It's so important to develop learning experiences that are perfect for your particular students, so have fun with this activity and don't be afraid to get creative.

ACTIVITY 8.5

Real Reviews! Writing Book Reviews for the School Library Catalog

In this activity, students have a chance to experience how much their opinions matter by writing online book reviews that can be viewed by anyone using your school district's library catalog. With the assistance of your school and public librarians, gather copies of professional book review journals, such as *School Library Journal*, *Booklist*, *Publishers Weekly*, *Kirkus Reviews*, and *The Horn Book*. Encourage students to find and read reviews of nonfiction books. They can compare these to reviews written by enthusiastic amateurs on sites like Goodreads (www.goodreads.com).

Next, students read a nonfiction book of their choice (any topic, any category) and write a book review, using the professional reviews as mentor texts. After a round of proofreading done in conjunction with the school librarian, students type their reviews into the school district's library catalog.

We have no doubt that the treasure trove of engaging ideas and activities in this chapter have left you feeling inspired and energized to explore, evaluate, and celebrate nonfiction with your students. The wide world of nonfiction has so much to offer young readers, and the 5 Kinds of Nonfiction classification system can help them navigate that world with ease.

And yet, the 5 Kinds of Nonfiction classification system isn't perfect. Some nonfiction books defy categorization because they feature characteristics of two or more categories. As you'll discover in Chapter 9, we're excited by these "blended books," especially the ones that include roughly equal amounts of narrative and expository text. Because blended books can bridge the gap between the captivating browseable books elementary students love and the more rigorous, long-form nonfiction they're required to read in middle school and high school, they can solve a problem that educators have been struggling with for decades.

"*Blended nonfiction is an unusual and unforgettable literary experience for young readers. It presents information in a way that piques readers' interest while expanding their base knowledge of a topic and challenging their minds.*"

—Terrence Young, Jr., retired school librarian; ALA Caldecott, Sibert, Edwards, and Morris Award committee member; and chair (2005-2019), AAAS/Subaru Prize for Excellence in Science Books committee

What Is Blended Nonfiction?

When we asked educators to try the 5 Kinds of Nonfiction book-sorting activity included at the beginning of Chapter 4 and submit their students' responses to us, we weren't sure what to expect. We had so many questions.

- Would students enjoy classifying books?
- Would they struggle to understand the characteristics of the various categories?
- Would they see the benefits of being able to identify a book's category?
- Would they have a strong preference for a particular category?

As the responses came in, we were delighted. Teachers and school librarians reported that their students were excited to think about nonfiction in this new way. Children as young as seven were able to sort books effectively, and most students could easily identify a favorite category. But there was one student comment in particular that blew us away.

Fifth graders sorting books using the 5 Kinds of Nonfiction classification system

"I think you should add an 'oddball' category. It's for books that are a mix of two or more categories." —Austin, fourth grader

Austin is right. Although most nonfiction children's books fit snugly into one specific category of the 5 Kinds of Nonfiction classification system, some titles are outliers. We call them "blended books" because they feature characteristics of two or more categories. We pay close attention to these category-crossing titles because they're direct evidence of innovation in action. Right now, this very minute, we're in the midst of a golden age of children's nonfiction. Each year, authors and illustrators are creating groundbreaking books that broaden our ideas about what nonfiction is and what it could become in the future.

In 2019, the year we're writing this book, author-illustrator Susan L. Roth produced an extraordinary children's book called *Birds of a Feather: Bowerbirds and Me*. Even though it's autobiographical, it's not narrative nonfiction. Instead, it's a fascinating expository meditation in which Roth explores her own creative process by comparing her artistic technique to the activities of a male bowerbird as he constructs a beautiful, extravagant structure to attract a mate. This incredible book is unlike anything we've ever seen before.

Also in 2019, author Mac Barnett published *The Important Thing About Margaret Wise Brown*, an astonishing picture book biography composed as a personal essay full of direct address that keeps readers engaged and involved. In the end, the innovative title is as much about Barnett's view of the world as it is about the life of the beloved children's book author of *Goodnight, Moon*, *Runaway Bunny*, and other classics.

While avant-garde titles like these can be tricky to categorize, knowing the 5 Kinds of Nonfiction classification system can enhance our ability to recognize and appreciate their craftsmanship and determine the best ways to use them in the classroom.

Other interesting examples of books that stretch and span categories include the Chicago Review Press For Kids series, which pairs biographical information about famous figures from the past with fun activities, and the popular National Geographic Readers series, which blurs the line between browseable books and traditional nonfiction.

We've also noticed some wonderful stand-alone titles that contain roughly equal amounts of expository and narrative text. The authors of these books move seamlessly from one writing style to the other, creating a blend of expository literature and narrative nonfiction that serves their subjects well. Turn the page for some great examples.

Giant Squid by Candace Fleming

The Great Monkey Rescue: Saving the Golden Lion Tamarins by Sandra Markle

How to Be an Elephant by Katherine Roy

Masters of Disguise: Amazing Animal Tricksters by Rebecca L. Johnson

Neighborhood Sharks: Hunting with the Great Whites of California's Farallon Islands by Katherine Roy

Sniffer Dogs: How Dogs (and Their Noses) Save the World by Nancy F. Castaldo

Snowy Owl Invasion!: Tracking an Unusual Migration by Sandra Markle

When Lunch Fights Back: Wickedly Clever Animal Defenses by Rebecca L. Johnson

Zombie Makers: True Stories of Nature's Undead by Rebecca L. Johnson

When evaluating blended books like these, it's sometimes useful to think of the five categories as touchstones or distinct points along a continuum, with adjacent categories intermingling. For example, some books combine characteristics of expository literature and narrative nonfiction. Others are a blend of browseable nonfiction and traditional nonfiction. In other cases, it's more helpful to envision a visual model with overlapping regions like a Venn diagram. For example, some books feature characteristics of active nonfiction and narrative nonfiction, while others are a mix of browseable nonfiction and expository literature. And still others blend characteristics of three categories.

We'll talk more about blended books, including their potential role in literacy development later in this chapter, but first, we think it's important to define and discuss another term that may be new to you—gateway nonfiction.

What Is Gateway Nonfiction?

Melissa first heard the term "gateway non-fiction" used by children's book author and nonfiction thought leader Marc Aronson in 2012. He attributes it to Jonathan Hunt, Coordinator of Library Media Services, San Diego, California. According to Hunt, gateway nonfiction is a theoretical group of books that can help students transition from the captivating browseable books they read with enthusiasm in elementary school to the more rigorous, long-form nonfiction they're expected to tackle in middle school and high school.

Aronson and Hunt believe that we need to clearly identify the characteristics of gateway nonfiction and then publish more of it. We wholeheartedly agree. After all, there's a lot at stake. While what's commonly known as the "fourth-grade slump" has been recognized by educators since the 1960s, the current focus on standardized testing has thrust the phenomenon into the limelight, causing greater concern than ever before (Springen 2007).

No one knows exactly what causes the declining interest in reading and gradual disengagement from school that many students experience between the end of the second grade and the middle of fifth grade, but we all acknowledge the need for solutions. And gateway nonfiction could be one of them. Just imagine how different things might be if educators could gently and gradually guide intermediate students across the reading chasm Hunt and Aronson have identified.

We believe that, for many students, blended titles that combine the key traits of expository literature and narrative nonfiction can serve as gateway nonfiction. Let's take a closer look at the nine exemplar titles we listed on page 140. All of these books focus on high-interest topics and are appropriate for readers in grades 3 to 6. They're well written, include stunning visuals, and have been designed with care.

The adorable golden lion tamarin on the cover of *The Great Monkey Rescue: Saving the Golden Lion Tamarins* by Sandra Markle is irresistible, and the content is just as compelling. Sandwiched between a gripping narrative beginning and a satisfying narrative ending, clear and engaging expository text with a Problem-Solution text structure describes how scientists and Brazilian community members worked together to save the endangered monkey from extinction. This is the kind of environmental success story that can inspire students and give them hope for the future.

Snowy Owl Invasion!: Tracking an Unusual Migration, also by Sandra Markle, shifts smoothly from one writing style to the other, allowing readers to follow the photogenic birds and the scientist studying them as they both experience a once-in-a-lifetime migratory event.

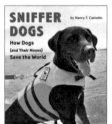

Sniffer Dogs: How Dogs (and Their Noses) Save the World by Nancy F. Castaldo is expository overall, but it makes expert use of occasional narrative sections about the author and her own beloved dog to reinforce specific points.

Neighborhood Sharks: *Hunting with the Great Whites of California's Farallon Islands* and *How to Be an Elephant,* both by Katherine Roy, include a fifty-fifty mix of narrative and expository text. Some spreads offer up-close scenes that show the animals in action, while others present rich expository descriptions and detailed diagrams of the animals' body features and how they function.

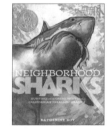

The three titles by Rebecca L. Johnson—*Masters of Disguise: Amazing Animal Tricksters, When Lunch Fights Back: Wickedly Clever Animal Defenses,* and *Zombie Makers: True Stories of Nature's Undead*—all make use of the same format to highlight fascinating predator–prey relationships from various perspectives. First, the author presents a riveting, action-packed narrative scene of the animals interacting. Then she follows up with an expository behind-the-story explanation of how the animals' behaviors help them survive—or not.

In all eight of the books mentioned earlier, the authors hook young readers with a narrative opening. It's a winning technique that works time and again. But in *Giant Squid*, Candace Fleming takes a different approach. She begins with a lyrical, luscious, wonderfully mysterious five-page expository opening that provides a general overview rather than focusing on a specific individual squid "character."  Only then does she plunge her readers into a gripping narrative scene that focuses on a single squid's fascinating feeding strategy. Was it the right decision? Absolutely!

Taken as a whole, *Giant Squid* is a fifty-fifty mix of three narrative scenes and gorgeous expository descriptions that do more than link one scene to the next. They bring readers into the life and the world of one of Earth's least known creatures. What a great book!

The Critical Role of Blended Nonfiction in Literacy Development

Why do we think blended books like these can bridge the gap between the titles that elementary readers love and the ones middle school students must be able to interact with? Why do we think they can engage and inform intermediate readers despite the fourth-grade reading slump? Because they have something for everyone, AND they can help all children build critical reading skills.

In Chapter 3, we shared research indicating that 25 percent of elementary students have a natural affinity for narratives, while 42 percent have a clear preference for expository writing and 33 percent enjoy both writing styles equally (Repaskey, Schumm, and Johnson 2017). The expository sections of high-quality, high-interest blended books will captivate fact-loving kids. The clear explanations and descriptions will feel comfortable and familiar to them, giving these students the confidence and motivation to tackle the narrative sections. And once these info-kids learn to access and enjoy narrative text, they can discover how characters—both real and imagined—exist in the world and successfully overcome challenges.

Similarly, young narrative lovers will be drawn to the story-rich sections of blended books, inspiring them to do the work necessary to digest and comprehend the expository passages. As a result, they'll be better equipped to wrangle the complex expository texts they'll encounter in middle school, high school, and college and in their future careers.

When students understand the 5 Kinds of Nonfiction, they can more easily identify the characteristics of blended nonfiction that match their natural reading preferences *and* learn to navigate the portions of the text outside their comfort zone. Approaching nonfiction in this way puts students in the driver's seat. It helps them understand their reading strengths and challenges, and it encourages them to stretch and grow as readers.

That's our end game. It's what we hope for all children . . . because before a child can become a confident, lifelong reader, they must first be able to successfully interact with a broad range of fiction and non-fiction texts.

Appendix A

Obtaining the Children's Books in This Guide

Although all of the children's books included in *5 Kinds of Nonfiction* were in print at the time of publication, that may no longer be true. If you discover that one of the books you'd like to use is no longer in print, don't worry. There are still many ways that you can locate copies.

- Check your school and public libraries. Even if they don't own the book, you may be able to obtain it through interlibrary loan.

- Check your local bookstore. Even if it's not in stock, the staff may be able to help you track it down.

- Try AbeBooks (www.abebooks.com), an online marketplace that can locate new, used, rare, and out-of-print books through a community of independent booksellers around the world.

- Check Alibris (www.alibris.com), which connects people with new, used, and hard-to-find books from thousands of independent sellers located all over the world.

- Search Amazon (www.amazon.com) to connect with sellers of used books. Enter the title of the book you seek, and see if any used copies are available.

- Check Powell's Books (www.powells.com), which offers an extensive list of both new and used books.

Appendix B
Resources for Finding High-Quality Nonfiction

Because many awards committee members have a natural preference for narrative writing, some prestigious awards consistently overlook exceptional expository titles. This underrepresentation can make it difficult to identify expository books that should be added to classroom and school library bookshelves. Fortunately, the sources listed below generally include a good mix of notable narrative and expository nonfiction.

- AAAS/Subaru Prizes for Excellence in Science Books
  www.sbfonline.com/Subaru/Pages/PastWinners.aspx

- California Reading Association Eureka! Nonfiction
  Children's Book Award
  www.juniorlibraryguild.com/awards/view.dT/state-awards
  /california/california-reading-association8217s-eureka
  -nonfiction-children8217s-book-awards

- Cook Prize for STEM Picture Book
  www.bankstreet.edu/center-childrens-literature/cook-prize

- Cooperative Children's Book Center Choices List
  ccbc.education.wisc.edu/books/choices.asp

- Cybils Nonfiction Awards
  www.cybils.com

- NCTE Orbis Pictus Award for Outstanding
  Nonfiction for Children
  www.ncte.org/awards/orbispictus

- NSTA-CBC Outstanding Science Trade Books
  for Students K–12
  www.nsta.org/publications/ostb

- Nerdy Book Club Book Nonfiction Awards
  nerdybookclub.wordpress.com

- Texas Topaz Nonfiction Reading List
  txla.org/tools-resources/reading-lists/texas-topaz/current-list

Appendix C
Activity Planner

To help you plan the activities in this book, the table below lists the children's books we recommend using. It also suggests appropriate grade levels for the activities. In many cases, the activities can be modified for younger and older children. Feel free to adapt them to meet the specific needs of your students, schedule, and classroom setup.

Activity	Recommended Children's Books (See bibliography for full citations.)	Suggested Grade Levels	Page Numbers
1.1: Comparing Narrative and Expository Nonfiction	*Red-Eyed Tree Frog* by Joy Cowley *Frog or Toad? How Do You Know?* by Melissa Stewart	K–8	7–9
4.1: Introducing the 5 Kinds of Nonfiction Children's Books	*City Hawk: The Story of Pale Male* by Megan McCarthy *Feathers: Not Just for Flying* by Melissa Stewart *Penguins* by Seymour Simon *Eyewitness Books: Bird* by David Burnie *National Geographic Kids Bird Guide of North America* by Jonathan Alderfer	2–8	40–42
4.2: Reinforcing the 5 Kinds of Nonfiction Children's Books	Books of your choice	3–8	42
4.3: Nonfiction Appreciation and Examination	Books of your choice	K–8	57–59

Activity	Recommended Children's Books (See bibliography for full citations.)	Suggested Grade Levels	Page Numbers
5.1: Text Feature Posters	HarperCollins Let's Read and Find Out series (titles published since 2015) National Geographic Readers series Enslow Zoom in on Animals series	K–2	63–64
5.2: Text Format in Browseable Books	*Eyewitness Books: Whales* by Vassili Papastavrou *Giant Squid* by Candace Fleming	3–6	66–69
5.3: Text Format in Expository Literature	*Where in the Wild? Camouflaged Creatures Concealed . . . and Revealed* by David M. Schwartz *Mama Built a Little Nest* by Jennifer Ward *An Egg Is Quiet* by Dianna Hutts Aston *How to Clean a Hippopotamus: A Look at Unusual Animal Partnerships* by Steve Jenkins and Robin Page	3–6	71–72
5.4: Interruption Construction Treasure Hunt	*Death Eaters: Meet Nature's Scavengers* by Kelly Milner Halls	4–8	74
5.5: Text Scaffolding Treasure Hunt	*Hedy Lamar's Double Life: Hollywood Legend and Brilliant Inventor* by Laurie Wallmark *Mario and the Hole in the Sky: How a Chemist Saved Our Planet* by Elizabeth Rusch	4–8	76–77

Activity	Recommended Children's Books (See bibliography for full citations.)	Suggested Grade Levels	Page Numbers
6.1: Introducing Text Structures with Q&A	*Do Sharks Glow in the Dark? . . . and Other Shark-tastic Questions* by Mary Kay Carson *If You Hopped Like a Frog* by David M. Schwartz *Birds of a Feather: Bowerbirds and Me* by Susan L. Roth	3–4	82–84
6.2: Same Topic, Different Text Structures	*Fanatical About Frogs* by Owen Davey *Frog or Toad? How Do You Know?* by Melissa Stewart *Frogs* by Nic Bishop *Frog Song* by Brenda Z. Guiberson *The Hidden Life of a Toad* by Doug Wechsler *A Place for Frogs* by Melissa Stewart *Red-Eyed Tree Frog* by Joy Cowley	4–8	85–86
6.3: Experimenting with Text Structures	*What Do You Do with a Tail Like This?* by Steve Jenkins and Robin Page	3–5	90–92
6.4: Same Text Structure, New Topic	*What Do You Do with a Tail Like This?* by Steve Jenkins and Robin Page Scholastic What If You Had series by Sandra Markle Enslow Animal Bodies Up Close series by Melissa Stewart	3–5	92–94
7.1: Exploring Voice in Nonfiction	*Pink Is for Blobfish: Discovering the World's Perfectly Pink Animals* by Jess Keating *A Butterfly Is Patient* by Dianna Hutts Aston	4–8	102–103

Activity	Recommended Children's Books (See bibliography for full citations.)	Suggested Grade Levels	Page Numbers
7.2: Appreciating Rich Language in Nonfiction	*Before She Was Harriet: The Story of Harriet Tubman* by Lesa Cline-Ransome *Frog Song* by Brenda Z. Guiberson *Giant Squid* by Candace Fleming *If You Find a Rock* by Peggy Christian *If You Hopped Like a Frog* by David M. Schwartz *Planting the Wild Garden* by Kathryn O. Galbraith *Squirrels Leap, Squirrels Sleep* by April Pulley Sayre *We Are Grateful: Otsaliheliga* by Traci Sorell	4–8	105–107
7.3: Exploring Point of View in Nonfiction	*Dinosaurs by the Numbers* by Steve Jenkins *If You Decide to Go to the Moon* by Faith McNulty *If You Hopped Like a Frog* by David M. Schwartz *Poet: The Remarkable Story of George Moses Horton* by Don Tate *The Scraps Book: Notes from a Colorful Life* by Lois Ehlert *This Is How We Do It: One Day in the Lives of Seven Kids from Around the World* by Matt LaMothe	4–8	111–112
7.4: Experimenting with Voice and Point of View	*The Deadliest Creature in the World* by Brenda Z. Guiberson *Sun: One in a Billion* by Stacey McAnulty	4–8	113–116
8.1: Creating Nonfiction Book Displays	Books of your students' choice	K–8	120

Activity	Recommended Children's Books (See bibliography for full citations.)	Suggested Grade Levels	Page Numbers
8.2: Student Book Talks	Books of your students' choice	2–8	122
8.3: Nonfiction Smackdown! Evaluating and Comparing Two Books	*Death Eaters: Meet Nature's Scavengers* by Kelly Milner Halls *Rotten: Vultures, Beetles, Slime and Nature's Other Decomposers* by Anita Sanchez *Dog Days of History: The Incredible Story of Our Best Friends* by Sarah Albee *Made for Each Other: Why Dogs and People Are the Perfect Partners* by Dorothy Hinshaw Patent *Eye Spy: Wild Ways Animals See the World* by Guillaume Duprat *What If You Had Animal Eyes?* by Sandra Markle *Flying Deep: Climb Inside Deep-Sea Submersible ALVIN* by Michelle Cusolito *Otis and Will Discover the Deep: The Record-Setting Dive of the Bathysphere* by Barb Rosenstock *A Seed Is the Start* by Melissa Stewart *Seeds Move* by Robin Page	3–8	132–133
8.4: Sibert Smackdown! Selecting an Award Winner	Books of your choice. Melissa posts suggestions on her blog each year.	3–8	134–135
8.5: Real Reviews! Writing Book Reviews for the School Library Catalog	Books of your students' choice	4–8	135–136

Appendix D

Reproducibles for Activities

ACTIVITIES 4.1 AND 4.2

Category Feature Cards

5 Kinds of Nonfiction: Enriching Reading and Writing Instruction with Children's Books by Melissa Stewart and Marlene Correia. Copyright © 2021. Taylor & Francis Group

---

Typical Features of
Browseable Nonfiction

- Eye-catching design, lavishly illustrated
- Short blocks of straightforward text
- Can be read cover to cover or by skipping around
- Great for shared reading
- Expository writing style
- Description text structure

Typical Features of
Expository Literature

- Focused topic presented creatively
- Strong voice and rich, engaging language
- Innovative format
- Carefully chosen text structure
- Expository writing style
- Books about specialized ideas, such as STEM concepts

Typical Features of
Traditional Nonfiction

- Survey (all-about) books
- Overview of a topic
- Often part of a large series
- Clear, straightforward language
- Expository writing style
- Description text structure

Typical Features of
Active Nonfiction

- Highly interactive and/or teaches skills for engaging in an activity
- How-to guides, field guides, cookbooks, craft books
- Clear, straightforward language
- Expository writing style

Typical Features of
Narrative Nonfiction

- Narrative writing style
- Tells a story or conveys an experience
- Real characters, scenes, dialogue, narrative arc
- Strong voice and rich, engaging language
- Chronological sequence structure
- Books about people (biographies), events, or processes

ACTIVITY 8.2

Planning a Book Talk, Grades 2-3

A great nonfiction book talk makes other people want to read the book.

1. Choose a book you love.

2. Mark your favorite pages with sticky notes, so you can find them easily.

3. Use the following sentence starters to plan what you will say:

- The title of my book is _____.

- The author is _____.

- My favorite things about this book is _____

  _____.

- The most interesting thing I learned is _____

  _____.

  (Show page.)
- Another thing I learned was _____

  _____.

  (Show page.)
- You should read this book because _____

  _____.

4. During the presentation, hold up the book so everyone can see it. Give your audience just enough information to make them curious.

Planning a Book Talk, Grades 4-8

5 Kinds of Nonfiction: Enriching Reading and Writing Instruction with Children's Books by Melissa Stewart and Marlene Correia. Copyright © 2021. Taylor & Francis Group

1. Choose a book you love.

2. Start by showing the cover of the book. Then read the title and the name of the book's author. If there is an illustrator, share their name too.

3. Next, use a hook that will capture your classmates' interest. It could be a great quotation from the book or an unusual picture. You could also start by asking a related question or making a connection to something in the news.

4. Briefly summarize the book without giving away too much information. The goal is to make your classmates curious.

5. Share the book's nonfiction category. Is it active, browseable, traditional, expository literature, or narrative?

6. Tell your classmates why you loved the book, and share at least two fascinating facts that you learned. (If you mark your favorite pages with sticky notes, they will be easier to find during your book talk.)

7. Explain why you think someone might want to read this book. (This can be general, but it can also be specific. For example, if you know a classmate who's interested in trains and your book is about trains then you might say, "I think Carly would like this book because . . .").

8. End with an encouraging statement (Example: Check out *Girls with Guts: The Road to Breaking Barriers and Bashing Records* by Debbie Gonzales to discover how women athletes have stunned the world by achieving goals nobody thought they could!)

ACTIVITY 8.3

Nonfiction Smackdown!
Evaluating and Comparing Two Books

Name: _____ Date: _____

Your mission is to read TWO different nonfiction books on the exact same topic and decide which one is best.

My books are about _____.

Use the table below to compare your books.

Put a check mark under the book that:	Book 1 Author and Title:	Book 2 Author and Title:
Has the most information about the topic		
Is easiest to understand		
Is the most interesting		
Has the best illustrations (photos, drawings, graphs, diagrams, maps)		
Has the most helpful text features (table of contents, glossary, headings)		

Now go back and circle the title of the best book on your topic. Then write a couple of juicy sentences below that describe how you would classify it, and explain why you'd recommend this book to someone who wants to know about the topic:

_____

_____

_____

Sibert Smackdown!
Selecting an Award Winner

Name: _____ Date: _____

Your mission is to read TWO different nonfiction books and decide which one should win the Sibert Medal. Use the table below to compare the books.

Put a check mark under the book that:	Book 1 Author and Title:	Book 2 Author and Title:
Has the most information about the topic		
Is the most interesting and easy to understand		
Includes craft moves like vivid verbs, rich language, strong voice		
Has the best illustrations (photos, drawings, graphs, diagrams, maps)		
Has the most helpful text features (table of contents, glossary, headings)		
Has the best back matter (sources, author's note, etc.)		

Now circle the title of the book you think is the best choice for the Sibert Medal.

What is the main idea of that book? _____

List two details that support the book's main idea.

1. _____

2. _____

Write a couple of juicy sentences recommending the book you chose to other people:

_____

_____

5 Kinds of Nonfiction: Enriching Reading and Writing Instruction with Children's Books by Melissa Stewart and Marlene Correia. Copyright © 2021. Taylor & Francis Group

Appendix E

Nonfiction Picture Books
That Are Perfect for Reading Aloud

While this list features a broad range of nonfiction titles, you'll notice that we haven't included any picture book biographies (which represent the majority of history/social studies and arts books being published today). That's because they tend to be longer books, and they need to be read cover to cover. These characteristics make them difficult to share within a typical read-aloud time frame.

Actual Size by Steve Jenkins

Because of an Acorn by Lola M. Schafer

Birds of a Feather: Bowerbirds and Me by Susan L. Roth

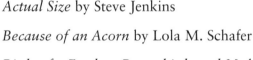

Born in the Wild: Baby Mammals and Their Parents by Lita Judge

Cute as an Axolotl: Discovering the World's Most Adorable Animals by Jess Keating[*]

Daylight Starlight Wildlife by Wendell Minor

Did You Burp? How to Ask Questions . . . or Not! by April Pulley Sayre

An Egg Is Quiet by Dianna Hutts Aston

Flip, Float, Fly: Seeds on the Move by JoAnn Early Macken

* These are longer picture books, but because each double-page spread is self-contained, it's easy to share just a few pages as a read aloud.

Flying Frogs and Walking Fish: Leaping Lemurs, Tumbling Toads, Jet-Propelled Jellyfish, and More Surprising Ways That Animals Move by Steve Jenkins and Robin Page*

Frog Song by Brenda Z. Guiberson

Giant Squid by Candace Fleming

Handimals: Animals in Art and Nature by Silvia Lopez*

How to Swallow a Pig: Step-by-Step Advice from the Animal Kingdom by Steve Jenkins and Robin Page*

A Hundred Billion Trillion Stars by Seth Fishman

If You Find a Rock by Peggy Christian

If You Hopped Like a Frog by David M. Schwartz

Mama Built a Little Nest by Jennifer Ward

Many: The Diversity of Life on Earth by Nicola Davies

Move! by Steve Jenkins & Robin Page

Mysterious Patterns: Finding Fractals in Nature by Sarah C. Campbell

Pipsqueaks, Slowpokes, and Stinkers: Celebrating Animal Underdogs by Melissa Stewart

Planting the Wild Garden by Kathryn O. Galbraith

Rodent Rascals by Roxie Munro

The Street Beneath My Feet by Charlotte Guillain

Stretch to the Sun: From a Tiny Sprout to the Tallest Tree on Earth by Carrie A. Pearson

Swirl by Swirl: Spirals in Nature by Joyce Sidman

Trout Are Made of Trees by April Pulley Sayre

Wait, Rest, Pause: Dormancy in Nature by Marcie Flinchum Atkins

Warbler Wave by April Pulley Sayre

Water Land: Land and Water Forms Around the World by Christy Hale

We Are Grateful: Otsaliheliga by Traci Sorell

Weeds Find a Way by Cindy Jenson-Elliott

With a Friend by Your Side by Barbara Kerley

Wolfsnail: A Backyard Predator by Sarah C. Campbell

The World Is Waiting for You by Barbara Kerley

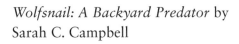

Bibliography of Children's Books

Chapter 1

Carson, Mary Kay. *Wildlife Ranger Action Guide: Track, Spot, & Provide Healthy Habitat for Creatures Close to Home.* North Adams, MA: Storey, 2020.

Cline-Ransome, Lesa. *Game Changers: The Story of Venus and Serena Williams.* New York: Simon & Schuster, 2018.

Cowley, Joy. *Red-Eyed Tree Frog.* New York: Scholastic, 1999.

Editors of TIME for Kids. *Big Book of WHY Revised and Updated.* New York: Time for Kids, 2016.

Frank, Sarah. *Golden Retrievers.* Minneapolis, MN: Lerner, 2019.

Greenberg, Jan, and Sandra Jordan. *Two Brothers, Four Hands.* New York: Holiday House, 2019.

Guinness World Records. *Guinness World Records 2020.* New York: Guinness World Records, 2019.

Jarrow, Gail. *Spooked! How a Radio Broadcast and* The War of the Worlds *Sparked the 1938 Invasion of America.* Honesdale, PA: Calkins Creek, 2018.

Newman, Patricia. *Sea Otter Heroes: The Predators That Saved an Ecosystem.* Minneapolis, MN: Millbrook, 2017.

Sorell, Traci. *We Are Grateful: Otsaliheliga.* Watertown, MA: Charlesbridge, 2018.

Stewart, Melissa. *Frog or Toad? How Do You Know?* New York: Enslow, 2011.

Chapter 2

Albee, Sarah. *North America: A Fold-Out Graphic History.* London: What on Earth Books, 2019.

Alderfer, Jonathan. *National Geographic Kids Bird Guide of North America: Second Edition.* Washington, DC: National Geographic, 2018.

Aston, Dianna Hutts. *A Butterfly Is Patient.* San Francisco: Chronicle, 2011.

Burns, Loree Griffin. *You're Invited to a Moth Ball: A Nighttime Insect Celebration*. Watertown, MA: Charlesbridge, 2020.

Carson, Mary Kay. *Wildlife Ranger Action Guide: Track, Spot, & Provide Healthy Habitat for Creatures Close to Home*. North Adams, MA: Storey, 2020.

Cook, Deanna F. *Cooking Class Global Feast! 44 Recipes That Celebrate the World's Cultures*. North Adams, MA: Storey, 2019.

Anika Aldamuy. *Planting Stories: The Life of Librarian and Storyteller Pura Belpré*. New York: HarperCollins, 2019.

Doeden, Matt. *Monster Trucks*. Mankato, MN: Capstone, 2018.

Drimmer, Stephanie Warren. *The Book of Queens: Legendary Leaders, Fierce Females, and Wonder Women Who Ruled the World*. Washington, DC: National Geographic, 2019.

Duprat, Guillaume. *Eye Spy: Wild Ways Animals See the World*. London: What on Earth Books, 2018.

Editors of TIME for Kids. *Big Book of WHY Revised and Updated*. New York: Time for Kids, 2016.

Frank, Sarah. *Golden Retrievers*. Minneapolis, MN: Lerner, 2019.

Gibbons, Gail. *Coral Reefs*. New York: Holiday House, 2019.

Greenberg, Jan, and Sandra Jordan. *Two Brothers, Four Hands*. New York: Holiday House, 2019.

Guinness World Records. *Guinness World Records 2020*. New York: Guinness World Records, 2019.

Ignotofsky, Rachel. *Women in Art: 50 Fearless Creatives Who Inspired the World*. Berkeley, CA: Ten Speed, 2019.

Jarrow, Gail. *Spooked! How a Radio Broadcast and* The War of the Worlds *Sparked the 1938 Invasion of America*. Honesdale, PA: Calkins Creek, 2018.

Judge, Lita. *Homes in the Wild: Where Baby Animals and Their Parents Live*. New York: Roaring Brook, 2019.

Lawrence, Blythe. *Behind the Scenes Gymnastics*. Minneapolis, MN: Lerner, 2019.

Markle, Sandra. *What If You Had* T. rex *Teeth? And Other Dinosaur Parts*. New York: Scholastic, 2019.

Masiello, Ralph. *Ralph Masiello's Alien Drawing Book*. Watertown, MA: Charlesbridge, 2019.

Messner, Kate. *The Next President: The Unexpected Beginnings and Unwritten Future of America's Presidents*. San Francisco, CA: Chronicle, 2020.

Nargi, Lela. *Karl's New Beak*. North Mantako, MN: Capstone, 2019.

Rissman, Rebecca. *Hair-Raising Hairstyles That Make a Statement*. Mankato, MN: Compass Point Books, 2018.

Sanchez, Anita. *Rotten: Vultures, Beetles, Slime and Nature's Other Decomposers*. Boston: Houghton Mifflin Harcourt, 2019.

Sills, Cathryn. *Rivers and Streams*. Atlanta: Peachtree, 2019.

Simon, Seymour. *Butterflies*. New York: HarperCollins, 2011.

Simon, Seymour. *Exoplanets*. New York: HarperCollins, 2018.

Sorell, Traci. *We Are Grateful: Otsaliheliga*. Watertown, MA: Charlesbridge, 2018.

Szymanski, Jennifer. *Code This! Puzzles, Games, Challenges, and Computer Coding Concepts for the Problem Solver in You*. Washington, DC: National Geographic, 2019.

Valdez, Patricia. *Joan Proctor, Reptile Doctor: The Woman Who Loved Reptiles*. New York: Knopf, 2018.

Weiss, Sabrina, and Giulia De Amicis. *Ocean: Secrets of the Deep*. London: What on Earth Books, 2019.

Chapter 3

Cowley, Joy. *Red-Eyed Tree Frog*. New York: Scholastic, 1999.

Kudlinski, Kathleen. *Boy, Were We Wrong About Dinosaurs!* New York: Dutton, 2008.

Stewart, Melissa. *Frog or Toad? How Do You Know?* New York: Enslow, 2011.

Chapter 4

Alderfer, Jonathan. *National Geographic Kids Bird Guide of North America: Second Edition*. Washington, DC: National Geographic, 2018.

Atkins, Marcie Flinchum. *Wait, Rest, Pause: Dormancy in Nature*. Minneapolis, MN: Millbrook, 2019.

Barretta Gene *Now & Ben: The Modern Inventions of Benjamin Franklin*. New York: Holt, 2008.

Burnie, David. *Eyewitness Books: Bird*. London: DK Children, 2008.

Drimmer, Stephanie Warren. *Ultimate Weather-pedia*. Washington, DC: National Geographic, 2019.

Jenson-Elliott, Cindy. *Weeds Find a Way*. San Diego: Beach Lane Books/Simon & Schuster, 2013.

McCarthy, Megan. *City Hawk: The Story of Pale Male*. New York: Simon & Schuster, 2007.

Miller, Brandon Marie. *Benjamin Franklin, American Genius: His Life and Ideas with 21 Activities*. Chicago: Chicago Review Press, 2009.

Simon, Seymour. *Penguins*. New York: HarperCollins, 2010.

Simon, Seymour. *Weather*. New York: HarperCollins, 2006.

Stewart, Melissa. *Feathers: Not Just for Flying*. Watertown, MA: Charlesbridge, 2014.

Chapter 5

Aston, Dianna Hutts. *An Egg Is Quiet*. San Francisco: Chronicle, 2006.

Fleming, Candace. *Giant Squid*. New York: Neal Porter Books/Roaring Brook, 2016.

Halls, Kelly Milner. *Death Eaters: Meet Nature's Scavengers*. Minneapolis, MN: Millbrook, 2018.

Jenkins, Steve, and Robin Page. *How to Clean a Hippopotamus: A Look at Unusual Animal Partnerships*. Boston: Houghton Mifflin Harcourt, 2010.

Jenkins, Steve, and Robin Page. *Move!* Boston: Houghton Mifflin Harcourt, 2006.

Keating, Jess. *Pink Is for Blobfish: Discovering the World's Perfectly Pink Animals*. New York: Knopf, 2016.

Markle, Sandra. *Snowy Owl Invasion!: Tracking an Unusual Migration*. Minneapolis, MN: Millbrook, 2018.

Papastavrou, Vassili. *Eyewitness Books: Whales*. London: DK Children, 2004.

Rusch, Elizabeth. *Mario and the Hole in the Sky: How a Chemist Saved Our Planet*. Watertown, MA: Charlesbridge, 2019.

Sanchez, Anita. *Itch! Everything You Didn't Want to Know About What Makes You Scratch*. Boston: Houghton Mifflin Harcourt, 2018.

Schwartz, David M. *Where in the Wild? Camouflaged Creatures Concealed . . . and Revealed*. Berkeley, CA: Tricycle Press, 2011.

Stewart, Melissa. *Ick! Delightfully Disgusting Animal Dinners, Dwellings, and Defenses*. Washington, DC: National Geographic, 2018.

Stewart, Melissa. *Zoom in on Bees*. Berkeley Heights, NJ: Enslow, 2014.

Swanson, Jennifer. *Super Gear: Nanotechnology and Sports Team Up*. Watertown, MA: Charlesbridge, 2016.

Wallmark, Laurie. *Hedy Lamarr's Double Life: Hollywood Legend and Brilliant Inventor*. New York: Sterling, 2019.

Ward, Jennifer. *Mama Built a Little Nest*. New York: Simon & Schuster, 2014.

Chapter 6

Albee, Sarah. *Bugged: How Insects Changed History*. New York, Bloomsbury, 2014.

Barretta, Gene. *Lincoln and Kennedy: A Pair to Compare*. New York: Holt, 2016.

Bishop, Nic. *Frogs*. New York: Scholastic, 2008.

Carson, Mary Kay. *Do Sharks Glow in the Dark? . . . and Other Shark-tastic Questions*. New York: Sterling, 2019.

Clinton, Chelsea. *She Persisted: 13 American Women Who Changed the World*. New York: Philomel, 2017.

Cowley, Joy. *Red-Eyed Tree Frog*. New York: Scholastic, 1999.

Davey, Owen. *Bonkers About Beetles*. London: Flying Eye Books, 2018.

Davey, Owen. *Fanatical About Frogs*. London: Flying Eye Books, 2019.

Davies, Nicola. *Many: The Diversity of Life on Earth*. Somerville, MA: Candlewick, 2017.

Fishman, Seth. *A Hundred Billion Trillion Stars*. New York: Greenwillow, 2017.

Guiberson, Brenda Z. *Earth: Feeling the Heat*. New York: Holt, 2010.

Guiberson, Brenda Z. *Feathered Dinosaurs*. New York: Holt, 2016.

Guiberson, Brenda Z. *Frog Song*. New York: Holt, 2013.

Jenkins, Steve. *Big & Little*. Boston: Houghton Mifflin Harcourt, 1996.

Jenkins, Steve. *The Frog Book*. Boston: Houghton Mifflin Harcourt, 2019.

Jenkins, Steve. *Look at Me! How to Attract Attention in the Animal World*. Boston: Houghton Mifflin Harcourt, 2018.

Jenkins, Steve. *Never Smile at a Monkey: And 17 Other Important Things to Remember*. Boston: Houghton Mifflin Harcourt, 2014.

Jenkins, Steve, and Robin Page. *How to Swallow a Pig: Step-by-Step Advice from the Animal Kingdom*. Boston: Houghton Mifflin Harcourt, 2015.

Jenkins, Steve, and Robin Page. *What Do You Do with a Tail Like This?* Boston: Houghton Mifflin Harcourt, 2003.

Judge, Lita. *Homes in the Wild: Where Baby Animals and Their Parents Live*. New York: Roaring Brook, 2019.

Keating, Jess. *Pink Is for Blobfish: Discovering the World's Perfectly Pink Animals*. New York: Knopf, 2016.

Kudlinski, Kathleen. *Boy, Were We Wrong About Dinosaurs!* New York: Dutton, 2008.

LaMothe, Matt. *This Is How We Do It: One Day in the Lives of Seven Kids from Around the World*. San Francisco: Chronicle, 2017.

Levine, Sara. *Bone by Bone: Comparing Animal Skeletons*. Minneapolis, MN: Millbrook, 2013.

Markle, Sandra. *The Great Monkey Rescue: Saving the Golden Lion Tamarins*. Minneapolis, MN: Millbrook, 2015.

Messner, Kate. *The Next President: The Unexpected Beginnings and Unwritten Future of America's Presidents*. San Francisco: Chronicle, 2020.

Minor, Wendell. *Daylight Starlight Wildlife*. New York: Nancy Paulsen Books/Penguin Random House, 2015.

Munro, Roxie. *Hatch!* New York: Two Lions, 2011.

Munro, Roxie. *Rodent Rascals*. New York: Holiday House, 2018.

Rockliff, Mara. *Mesmerized: How Ben Franklin Solved a Mystery That Baffled All of France*. Somerville, MA: Candlewick, 2015.

Roth, Susan L. *Birds of a Feather: Bowerbirds and Me*. New York: Neal Porter Books/Holiday House, 2019.

Sayre, April Pulley. *Trout Are Made of Trees*. Watertown, MA: Charlesbridge, 2008.

Schwartz, David M. *If You Hopped like a Frog*. New York: Scholastic, 1999.

Sidman, Joyce. *Swirl by Swirl: Spirals in Nature*. Boston: Houghton Mifflin Harcourt, 2011.

Sorell, Traci. *We Are Grateful: Otsaliheliga*. Watertown, MA: Charlesbridge, 2018.

Stewart, Melissa. *Can an Aardvark Bark?* New York: Simon & Schuster, 2017.

Stewart, Melissa. *Frog or Toad? How Do You Know?* New York: Enslow, 2011.

Stewart, Melissa. *A Place for Frogs*. Atlanta: Peachtree, 2016.

Wechsler, Doug. *The Hidden Life of a Toad*. Watertown, MA: Charlesbridge, 2017.

Williams, Lily. *If Sharks Disappeared*. New York: Roaring Brook Press, 2017.

Chapter 7

Albee, Sarah. *North America: A Fold-Out Graphic History*. London: What on Earth Books, 2019.

Albee, Sarah. *Poison: Deadly Deeds, Perilous Professions, and Murderous Medicines*. New York: Crown, 2017.

Aston, Dianna Hutts. *A Butterfly Is Patient*. San Francisco: Chronicle, 2011.

Barnett, Mac. *The Important Thing About Margaret Wise Brown.* New York: Balzer and Bray, 2019.

Burleigh, Robert. *Solving the Puzzle Under the Sea: Marie Tharp Maps the Ocean Floor.* New York: Paula Wiseman Books/Simon & Schuster, 2016.

Christian, Peggy. *If You Find a Rock.* Boston: Houghton Mifflin Harcourt, 2000.

Cline-Ransome, Lesa. *Before She Was Harriet: The Story of Harriet Tubman.* New York: Holiday House, 2017.

Cusolito, Michelle. *Flying Deep: Climb Inside Deep-Sea Submersible ALVIN.* Watertown, MA: Charlesbridge, 2018.

Davies, Nicola. *Tiny Creatures: The World of Microbes.* Sommerville, MA: Candlewick, 2014.

Doeden, Matt. *Monster Trucks.* Mankato, MN: Capstone, 2018.

Ehlert, Lois. *The Scraps Book: Notes from a Colorful Life.* San Diego: Beach Lane Books/Simon & Schuster, 2014.

Fleming, Candace. *Giant Squid.* New York: Neal Porter Books/ Roaring Brook, 2016.

Galbraith, Kathryn. *Planting the Wild Garden.* Atlanta: Peachtree, 2011.

Guiberson, Brenda Z. *The Deadliest Creature in the World.* New York: Holt, 2016.

Guiberson, Brenda Z. *Frog Song.* New York: Holt, 2013.

Heos, Bridget. I, Fly: *The Buzz About Flies and How Awesome They Are.* New York: Holt, 2015.

Jenkins, Steve. *Dinosaurs by the Numbers.* Boston: Houghton Mifflin Harcourt, 2019.

Keating, Jess. *Pink Is for Blobfish: Discovering the World's Perfectly Pink Animals.* New York: Knopf, 2016.

Krosoczka, Jarrett. *Hey, Kiddo.* New York: Graphix/Scholastic, 2018.

LaMothe, Matt. *This Is How We Do It: One Day in the Lives of Seven Kids from Around the World.* San Francisco: Chronicle, 2017.

Levine, Sara. *Bone by Bone: Comparing Animal Skeletons.* Minneapolis, MN: Millbrook, 2013.

McAnulty, Stacey. *Sun: One in a Billion*. New York: Holt, 2018.

McNulty, Faith. *If You Decide to Go to the Moon*. New York: Scholastic, 2005.

Meltzer, Brad. *I Am Rosa Parks*. New York: Dial, 2014.

Montgomery, Heather L. *Something Rotten: A Fresh Look at Roadkill*. New York: Bloomsbury, 2018.

Pearson, Carrie A. *Stretch to the Sun: From a Tiny Sprout to the Tallest Tree on Earth*. Watertown, MA: Charlesbridge, 2018.

Poliquin, Rachel. *Beavers: The Superpower Field Guide*. Boston: Houghton Mifflin Harcourt, 2018.

Portis, Antoinette. *Hey, Water*. New York: Neal Porter Books/ Holiday House, 2019.

Roth, Susan L. *Birds of a Feather: Bowerbirds and Me*. New York: Neal Porter Books/Holiday House, 2019.

Sanchez, Anita. *Itch! Everything You Didn't Want to Know About What Makes You Scratch*. Boston: Houghton Mifflin Harcourt, 2018.

Sayre, April Pulley. *Squirrels Leap, Squirrels Sleep*. New York: Holt, 2016.

Schwartz, David M. *If You Hopped Like a Frog*. New York: Scholastic, 1999.

Siegel, Randy. *One Proud Penny*. New York: Neal Porter Books/ Roaring Brook, 2017.

Sorell, Traci. *We Are Grateful: Otsaliheliga*. Watertown, MA: Charlesbridge, 2018.

Tate, Don. *Poet: The Remarkable Story of George Moses Horton*. Atlanta: Peachtree, 2015.

Woodson, Jacqueline. *Brown Girl Dreaming*. New York: Nancy Paulsen Books/Penguin Random House, 2014.

Chapter 8

Albee, Sarah. *Dog Days of History: The Incredible Story of Our Best Friends*. Washington, DC: National Geographic, 2018.

Aston, Dianna Hutts. *An Egg Is Quiet*. San Francisco: Chronicle, 2006.

Cline-Ransome, Lesa. *Before She Was Harriet: The Story of Harriet Tubman.* New York: Holiday House, 2017.

Cline-Ransome, Lesa. *Game Changers: The Story of Venus and Serena Williams.* New York: Simon & Schuster, 2018.

Clinton, Chelsca. *She Persisted: 13 American Women Who Changed the World.* New York: Philomel, 2017.

Cusolito, Michelle. *Flying Deep: Climb Inside Deep-Sea Submersible ALVIN.* Watertown, MA: Charlesbridge, 2018.

Danneberg, Julie. *First Day Jitters.* Watertown, MA: Charlesbridge, 2000.

Duprat, Guillaume. *Eye Spy: Wild Ways Animals See the World.* London: What on Earth Books, 2018.

Fleming, Candace. *Giant Squid.* New York: Neal Porter Books/ Roaring Brook, 2016.

Halls, Kelly Milner. *Death Eaters: Meet Nature's Scavengers.* Minneapolis, MN: Millbrook, 2018.

Jenkins, Steve, and Robin Page. *Flying Frogs and Walking Fish: Leaping Lemurs, Tumbling Toads, Jet-Propelled Jellyfish, and More Surprising Ways That Animals Move.* Boston: Houghton Mifflin Harcourt, 2016.

Keating, Jess. *Cute as an Axolotl: Discovering the World's Most Adorable Animals.* New York: Knopf, 2019.

Kerley. Barbara. *One World, One Day.* Washington, DC: National Geographic, 2009.

LaMothe, Matt. *This Is How We Do It: One Day in the Lives of Seven Kids from Around the World.* San Francisco: Chronicle, 2017.

Markle, Sandra. *What If You Had Animal Ears?* New York: Scholastic, 2016.

Markle, Sandra. *What If You Had Animal Eyes?* New York: Scholastic, 2017.

Page, Robin. *Seeds Move.* San Diego: Beach Lane Books/Simon & Schuster, 2019.

Patent, Dorothy Hinshaw. *Made for Each Other: Why Dogs and People Are the Perfect Partners.* New York: Crown, 2018.

Rex, Adam. *School's First Day of School*. New York: Roaring Brook, 2016.

Rosenstock, Barb. *Otis and Will Discover the Deep: The Record-Setting Dive of the Bathysphere*. New York: Little, Brown, 2018.

Roth, Susan L. *Birds of a Feather: Bowerbirds and Me*. New York: Neal Porter Books/Holiday House, 2019.

Sanchez, Anita. *Rotten: Vultures, Beetles, Slime and Nature's Other Decomposers*. Boston: Houghton Mifflin Harcourt, 2019.

Sayre, April Pulley. *Squirrels Leap, Squirrels Sleep*. New York: Holt, 2016.

Sayre, April Pulley. *Trout Are Made of Trees*. Watertown, MA: Charlesbridge, 2008.

Sayre, April Pulley. *Warbler Wave*. San Diego: Beach Lane Books/Simon & Schuster, 2018.

Schwartz, David M. *If You Hopped Like a Frog*. New York: Scholastic, 1999.

Sidman, Joyce. *Swirl by Swirl: Spirals in Nature*. Boston: Houghton Mifflin Harcourt, 2011.

Stewart, Melissa. *Pipsqueaks, Slowpokes, and Stinkers: Celebrating Animal Underdogs*. Atlanta: Peachtree, 2018.

Stewart, Melissa. *A Seed Is the Start*. Washington, DC: National Geographic, 2018.

Van Dusen, Chris. *If I Built a School*. New York: Dial, 2019.

Woodson, Jacqueline. *The Day You Begin*. New York: Nancy Paulsen Books/Penguin Random House, 2018.

Chapter 9

Barnett, Mac. *The Important Thing About Margaret Wise Brown*. New York: Balzer & Bray, 2019.

Brown, Margaret Wise. *Goodnight, Moon*. New York: HarperCollins, 2007.

Brown, Margaret Wise. *Runaway Bunny*. New York: HarperCollins, 2017.

Castaldo, Nancy F. *Sniffer Dogs: How Dogs (and Their Noses) Save the World*. Boston: Houghton Mifflin Harcourt, 2014.

Fleming, Candace. *Giant Squid*. New York: Neal Porter Books/
 Roaring Brook, 2016.

Markle, Sandra. *The Great Monkey Rescue: Saving the Golden Lion
 Tamarins*. Minneapolis, MN: Millbrook, 2015.

Markle, Sandra. *Snowy Owl Invasion!: Tracking an Unusual
 Migration*. Minneapolis, MN: Millbrook, 2018.

Johnson, Rebecca L. *Masters of Disguise: Amazing Animal
 Tricksters*. Minneapolis, MN: Millbrook, 2016.

Johnson, Rebecca L. *When Lunch Fights Back: Wickedly Clever
 Animal Defenses*. Minneapolis, MN: Millbrook, 2014.

Johnson, Rebecca L. *Zombie Makers: True Stories of Nature's
 Undead*. Minneapolis, MN: Millbrook, 2012.

Roth, Susan L. *Birds of a Feather: Bowerbirds and Me*. New York:
 Neal Porter Books/Holiday House, 2019.

Roy, Katherine. *How to Be an Elephant*. New York: David
 Macaulay Studio/Roaring Brook, 2017.

Roy, Katherine. *Neighborhood Sharks: Hunting with the Great
 Whites of California's Farallon Islands*. New York: David
 Macaulay Studio/Roaring Brook, 2014.

Appendix C

Albee, Sarah. *Dog Days of History: The Incredible Story of Our
 Best Friends*. Washington, DC: National Geographic, 2018.

Alderfer, Jonathan. *National Geographic Kids Bird Guide of
 North America: Second Edition*. Washington, DC: National
 Geographic, 2018.

Aston, Dianna Hutts. *A Butterfly Is Patient*. San Francisco:
 Chronicle, 2011.

Aston, Dianna Hutts. *An Egg Is Quiet*. San Francisco, CA:
 Chronicle, 2006.

Bishop, Nic. *Frogs*. New York: Scholastic, 2008.

Burnie, David. *Eyewitness Books: Bird*. London: DK Children,
 2008.

Carson, Mary Kay. *Do Sharks Glow in the Dark? . . . and Other
 Shark-tastic Questions*. New York: Sterling, 2019.

Christian, Peggy. *If You Find a Rock*. Boston: Houghton Mifflin Harcourt, 2000.

Cline-Ransome, Lesa. *Before She Was Harriet: The Story of Harriet Tubman*. New York: Holiday House, 2017.

Cowley, Joy. *Red-Eyed Tree Frog*. New York: Scholastic, 1999.

Cusolito, Michelle. *Flying Deep: Climb Inside Deep-Sea Submersible ALVIN*. Watertown, MA: Charlesbridge, 2018.

Davey, Owen. *Fanatical About Frogs*. London: Flying Eye Books, 2019.

Duprat, Guillaume. *Eye Spy: Wild Ways Animals See the World*. London: What on Earth Books, 2018.

Ehlert, Lois. *The Scraps Book: Notes from a Colorful Life*. San Diego: Beach Lane Books/Simon & Schuster, 2014.

Fleming, Candace. *Giant Squid*. New York: Neal Porter Books/Roaring Brook, 2016.

Galbraith, Kathryn. *Planting the Wild Garden*. Atlanta: Peachtree, 2011.

Guiberson, Brenda Z. *The Deadliest Creature in the World*. New York: Holt, 2016.

Guiberson, Brenda Z. *Frog Song*. New York: Holt, 2013.

Halls, Kelly Milner. *Death Eaters: Meet Nature's Scavengers*. Minneapolis, MN: Millbrook, 2018.

Jenkins, Steve. *Dinosaurs by the Numbers*. Boston: Houghton Mifflin Harcourt, 2019.

Jenkins, Steve, and Robin Page. *How to Clean a Hippopotamus: A Look at Unusual Animal Partnerships*. Boston: Houghton Mifflin Harcourt, 2010.

Jenkins, Steve, and Robin Page. *What Do You Do with a Tail Like This?* Boston: Houghton Mifflin Harcourt, 2003.

Keating, Jess. *Pink Is for Blobfish: Discovering the World's Perfectly Pink Animals*. New York: Knopf, 2016.

LaMothe, Matt. *This Is How We Do It: One Day in the Lives of Seven Kids from Around the World*. San Francisco: Chronicle, 2017.

Markle, Sandra. *What If You Had Animal Eyes?* New York: Scholastic, 2017.

McAnulty, Stacey. *Sun: One in a Billion*. New York: Holt, 2018.

McCarthy, Megan. *City Hawk: The Story of Pale Male*. New York: Simon & Schuster, 2007.

McNulty, Faith. *If You Decide to Go to the Moon*. New York: Scholastic, 2005.

Page, Robin. *Seeds Move*. San Diego: Beach Lane Books/Simon & Schuster, 2019.

Papastavrou, Vassili. *Eyewitness Books: Whales*. London: DK Children, 2004.

Patent, Dorothy Hinshaw. *Made for Each Other: Why Dogs and People Are the Perfect Partners*. New York: Crown, 2018.

Rosenstock, Barb. *Otis and Will Discover the Deep: The Record-Setting Dive of the Bathysphere*. New York: Little, Brown, 2018.

Roth, Susan L. *Birds of a Feather: Bowerbirds and Me*. New York: Neal Porter Books/Holiday House, 2019.

Rusch, Elizabeth. *Mario and the Hole in the Sky: How a Chemist Saved Our Planet*. Watertown, MA: Charlesbridge, 2019.

Sanchez, Anita. *Rotten: Vultures, Beetles, Slime and Nature's Other Decomposers*. Boston: Houghton Mifflin Harcourt, 2019.

Sayre, April Pulley. *Squirrels Leap, Squirrels Sleep*. New York: Holt, 2016.

Schwartz, David M. *If You Hopped Like a Frog*. New York: Scholastic, 1999.

Schwartz, David M. *Where in the Wild? Camouflaged Creatures Concealed . . . and Revealed*. Berkeley, CA: Tricycle Press, 2011.

Simon, Seymour. *Penguins*. New York: HarperCollins, 2010.

Sorell, Traci. *We Are Grateful: Otsaliheliga*. Watertown, MA: Charlesbridge, 2018.

Stewart, Melissa. *Feathers: Not Just for Flying*. Watertown, MA: Charlesbridge, 2014.

Stewart, Melissa. *Frog or Toad? How Do You Know?* New York: Enslow, 2011.

Stewart, Melissa. *A Place for Frogs*. Atlanta: Peachtree, 2016.

Stewart, Melissa. *A Seed Is the Start*. Washington, DC: National Geographic, 2018.

Tate, Don. *Poet: The Remarkable Story of George Moses Horton.* Atlanta: Peachtree, 2015.

Wallmark, Laurie. *Hedy Lamarr's Double Life: Hollywood Legend and Brilliant Inventor.* New York: Sterling, 2019.

Ward, Jennifer. *Mama Built a Little Nest.* San Diego: Beach Lane Books/Simon & Schuster, 2014.

Wechsler, Doug. *The Hidden Life of a Toad.* Watertown, MA: Charlesbridge, 2017.

Appendix D

Gonzales, Debbie. *Girls with Guts: The Road to Breaking Barriers and Bashing Records.* Watertown, MA: Charlesbridge, 2019.

Appendix E

Aston, Dianna Hutts. *An Egg Is Quiet.* San Francisco: Chronicle, 2006.

Atkins, Marcie Flinchum. *Wait, Rest, Pause: Dormancy in Nature.* Minneapolis, MN: Millbrook, 2019.

Campbell, Sarah C. *Mysterious Patterns: Finding Fractals in Nature.* Honesdale, PA: Boyds Mills Press, 2014.

Campbell, Sarah C. *Wolfsnail: A Backyard Predator.* Honesdale, PA: Boyds Mills Press, 2008.

Christian, Peggy. *If You Find a Rock.* Boston: Houghton Mifflin Harcourt, 2000.

Davies, Nicola. *Many: The Diversity of Life on Earth.* Somerville, MA: Candlewick, 2017.

Fishman, Seth. *A Hundred Billion Trillion Stars.* New York: Greenwillow, 2017.

Fleming, Candace. *Giant Squid.* New York: Neal Porter Books/Roaring Brook, 2016.

Galbraith, Kathryn. *Planting the Wild Garden.* Atlanta: Peachtree, 2011.

Guiberson, Brenda Z. *Frog Song.* New York: Holt, 2013.

Guillain, Charlotte. *The Street Beneath My Feet.* London: words & pictures, 2017.

Hale, Christy. *Water Land: Land and Water Forms Around the World*. New York: Neal Porter Books/Roaring Brook, 2018.

Jenkins, Steve. *Actual Size*. Boston: Houghton Mifflin Harcourt, 2014.

Jenkins, Steve, and Robin Page. *Flying Frogs and Walking Fish: Leaping Lemurs, Tumbling Toads, Jet-Propelled Jellyfish, and More Surprising Ways That Animals Move*. Boston: Houghton Mifflin Harcourt, 2016.

Jenkins, Steve, and Robin Page. *How to Swallow a Pig: Step-by-Step Advice from the Animal Kingdom*. Boston: Houghton Mifflin Harcourt, 2015.

Jenkins, Steve, and Robin Page. *Move!* Boston: Houghton Mifflin Harcourt, 2006.

Jenson-Elliott, Cindy. *Weeds Find a Way*. San Diego: Beach Lane Books/Simon & Schuster, 2013.

Judge, Lita. *Born in the Wild: Baby Mammals and Their Parents*. New York: Roaring Brook, 2014.

Keating, Jess. *Cute as an Axolotl: Discovering the World's Most Adorable Animals*. New York: Knopf, 2019.

Kerley, Barbara. *With a Friend by Your Side*. Washington, DC: National Geographic, 2015.

Kerley, Barbara. *The World Is Waiting for You*. Washington, DC: National Geographic, 2013.

Lopez. Silvia. *Handimals: Animals in Art and Nature*. New York: Holt, 2019.

Macken, JoAnn Early. *Flip, Float, Fly: Seeds on the Move*. New York: Holiday House, 2008.

Minor, Wendell. *Daylight Starlight Wildlife*. New York: Nancy Paulsen Books/Penguin Random House, 2015.

Munro, Roxie. *Rodent Rascals*. New York: Holiday House, 2018.

Pearson, Carrie A. *Stretch to the Sun: From a Tiny Sprout to the Tallest Tree on Earth*. Watertown, MA: Charlesbridge, 2018.

Roth, Susan L. *Birds of a Feather: Bowerbirds and Me*. New York: Neal Porter Books/Holiday House, 2019.

Sayre, April Pulley. *Did You Burp? How to Ask Questions . . . or Not!* Watertown, MA: Charlesbridge, 2019.

Sayre, April Pulley. *Trout Are Made of Trees*. Watertown, MA: Charlesbridge, 2008.

Sayre, April Pulley. *Warbler Wave*. San Diego: Beach Lane Books/Simon & Schuster, 2018.

Schafer, Lola M. *Because of an Acorn*. San Francisco: Chronicle, 2017.

Schwartz, David M. *If You Hopped Like a Frog*. New York: Scholastic, 1999.

Sidman, Joyce. *Swirl by Swirl: Spirals in Nature*. Boston: Houghton Mifflin Harcourt, 2011.

Sorell, Traci. *We Are Grateful: Otsaliheliga*. Watertown, MA: Charlesbridge, 2018.

Stewart, Melissa. *Pipsqueaks, Slowpokes, and Stinkers: Celebrating Animal Underdogs*. Atlanta: Peachtree, 2018.

Ward, Jennifer. *Mama Built a Little Nest*. San Diego: Beach Lane Books/Simon & Schuster, 2014.

Professional References

Notes from the Authors

Correia, M. 2011. "Fiction vs. Informational Texts: Which Will Your Kindergarteners Choose?" *Young Children* 66 (6): 100–104.

Jobe, R., and M. Dayton-Sakari. 2002. *Infokids: How to Use Nonfiction to Turn Reluctant Readers into Enthusiastic Learners*. Markham, Ontario, Canada: Pembroke.

Chapter 1

Aronson, M. 2016, March 21. "The Writer's Page: What Is Narrative Nonfiction?" *The Horn Book*. Retrieved from http://www.hbook.com/2016/03/choosing-books/horn-book-magazine/the-writers-page-what-is-narrative-nonfiction/.

Association for Library Service for Children. Robert F. Silbert Informational Book Award Terms and Criteria, 2015. Retrieved from http://www.ala.org/alsc/awardsgrants/bookmedia/sibertmedal/sibertterms/sibertmedaltrms.

Comaromi, J. P. 1976. *The Eighteen Editions of the Dewey Decimal Classification*. Albany, NY: Forest Press Division, Lake Placid Education Foundation.

Fleming, C. 2015, August. "Ten Secrets of Writing Narrative Nonfiction." Society of Children's Book Writers and Illustrators Annual Summer Conference, Los Angeles, CA.

May, L., T. Crisp, G. Bingham, R. Schwartz, M. Pickens, and K. Woodbridge. 2019, September. "The Durable, Dynamic Nature of Genre and Science: A Purpose-Driven Typology of Science Trade Books." *Reading Research Quarterly*, 1–20.

National Governors Association Center for Best Practices and Council of Chief State School Officers (NGAC and CCSSO). 2010. *Common Core State Standards for English Language Arts and Literacy in History/Social Studies, Science, and Technical Subjects*. Washington, DC.

Online Entomology Dictionary. ND. Retrieved from https://www.etymonline.com/word/Fiction.

Pappas, C. C. 1986, December. "Exploring the Global Structure of 'Information Books.'" Annual Meeting of the National Reading Conference, Austin, TX.

———. 1987, August. "Exploring the Generic Shape of 'Information Books': Applying Typicality Notions to the Process." World Conference of Applied Linguistics, Sydney, New South Wales, Australia.

Paradis, J. 2015. School librarian, Plympton Elementary School, Waltham, MA, and past president, Massachusetts School Library Association. Personal communication. September 26.

Schiesman, M. 2016. Librarian, Cooperative Children's Book Center of the School of Education at the University of Wisconsin-Madison, Personal communication. August 4.

Chapter 2

Emmett, J. 2012, November. "Explore Your World: Crafting Today's Nonfiction for Kids." Society of Children's Book Writers and Illustrators Eastern Upstate Chapter's Falling Leaves Masterclass Writing Retreat, Silver Bay, New York.

Hepler, S. 1998. "Nonfiction Books for Children: New Directions, New Challenges." In *Making Facts Come Alive: Choosing and Using Quality Nonfiction Literature K–9*, ed. R. A. Bamford and J. V. Kristo (3–20). 2nd ed. Norwood, MA: Christopher-Gordon.

Kachel, D. E., and K. C. Lance. 2013, March 7. "Latest Study: A Full-Time School Librarian Makes a Critical Difference in Boosting Student Achievement." *School Library Journal*. Retrieved from https://www.slj.com/?detailStory=librarian-required-a-new-study -shows-that-a-full-time-school-librarian-makes-a-critical-difference -in-boosting-student-achievement.

Kiefer, B. Z. 2010. *Charlotte Huck's Children's Literature*. Boston, MA: McGraw-Hill.

Kirkland, T. 2019. Personal communication. April 30.

Lodge, S. 1996. "Giving Kids' Reference a Fresh Look." *Publishers Weekly* 243 (18): 42–43.

Oxford English Dictionary. ND. Retrieved from http://www.oxford
dictionaries.com/us/definition/american_english/literature.

Rosen, J. 2017, January 30. "Separating Fact from Fiction." *Publishers
Weekly*, 16–18.

Stewart, M. 2013, May 8. "A Whole New Nonfiction Family Tree."
Celebrate Science. Retrieved from http://celebratescience.blogspot.
com/2013/05/behind-books-whole-new-nonfiction.html.

———. 2015, December 21. "Diversity in Thinking." *A Fuse #8
Production/School Library Journal*. Retrieved from *http://blogs.slj
.com/afuse8production/2015/12/21/guest-post-melissa-stewart
-and-diversity-in-thinking/#_*.

Stewart, M., and T. A. Young. 2018. "Defining and Describing
Expository Literature." In *Does Nonfiction Equate Truth?
Rethinking Disciplinary Boundaries Through Critical Literacies*,
ed. V. Yenika-Agbaw, R. M. Lowery, and L. A. Hudock (11–24).
Lanham, MD: Rowman and Littlefield.

———. 2019. "Teaching the Key Traits of Expository Nonfiction with
Children's Books." *The Reading Teacher* 72 (5): 648–651.

Tuck, K. D., and D. R. Holmes. 2016. "Library/Media Centers in
U.S. Public Schools: Growth, Staffing, and Resources." National
Education Association. Retrieved from http://www.nea.org
/home/67686.htm.

Chapter 3

American Library Association Youth Media Awards. Retrieved from
http://www.ala.org/awardsgrants/awards/browse/yma?showfilter=no.

Beck, I., M. McKeown, and L. Kucan. 2013. *Bringing Words to Life:
Robust Vocabulary Instruction*. 2nd ed. New York: Guilford Press.

Beers, K., and R. E. Probst. 2016. *Reading Nonfiction: Notice and Note
Stances, Signposts, and Strategies*. Portsmouth, NH: Heinemann.

Bukowiecki, E., and M. Correia. 2017. *Informational Texts in Pre-
Kindergarten Through Grade-Three Classrooms*. Lanham, MD:
Rowman and Littlefield.

Cambria, J., and J. T. Guthrie. 2010. "Motivating and Engaging Students
in Reading." *The New England Reading Association Journal* 46
(1): 16–29.

Correia, M. 2011. "Fiction vs. Informational Texts: Which Will Your Kindergarteners Choose?" *Young Children* 66 (6): 100–104.

Dreher, M. J., and S. Kletzien. 2015. *Teaching Informational Texts in K–3 Classrooms: Best Practices to Help Children Read, Write, and Learn from Nonfiction*. New York: Guilford.

Doiron, R. 2003. "Boy Books, Girl Books: Should We Reorganize Our School Library Collections?" *Teacher Librarian*, 14–16.

Duke, N. 2014. *Inside Information: Developing Powerful Readers and Writers of Informational Text Through Project-Based Instruction*. New York: Scholastic.

Duke, N. K., V. S. Bennett-Armistead, and E. M. Robert. 2003. "Bridging the Gap Between Learning to Read and Reading to Learn." In *Literacy and Young Children: Research-based Practices*, ed. D. M. Barone and L. M. Morrow (226–242). New York: Guilford.

Harvey, S., and A. Ward. 2017. *From Striving to Thriving: How to Grow Confident, Capable Readers*. New York: Scholastic.

Hirsch, E., and L. Hansel. 2013. "Why Content Is King." *Educational Leadership* 71 (3): 28–33.

Jobe, R., and M. Dayton-Sakari. 2002. *Infokids: How to Use Nonfiction to Turn Reluctant Readers into Enthusiastic Learners*. Markham, Ontario, Canada: Pembroke.

Maloch, B., and Horsey, M. 2013. "Living Inquiry: Learning from and About Informational Texts in a Second-Grade Classroom." *Reading Teacher* 66 (6): 475–485.

Mohr, K. 2006. "Children's Choices for Recreational Reading: A Three-Part Investigation of Select Preferences, Rationales, and Processes." *Journal of Literacy Research* 38 (1): 81–104.

Moss, B. 2008. "The Information Text Gap: The Mismatch Between Non-Narrative Text Types in Basal Readers and 2009 NAEP Recommended Guidelines." *Journal of Literacy Research* 40 (2): 201–219.

Moss, B., and J. Hendershot. 2002. "Exploring Sixth Graders' Selection of Nonfiction Trade Books." *Reading Teacher* 66 (1): 6–17.

Mullis, I. V. S., M. O. Martin, P. Foy, and K. T. Drucker. 2012. *PIRLS International Results in Reading*. Chestnut Hill, MA: TIMSS and PIRLS International Study Center/Boston College.

Pappas, C. C. 1991. "Fostering Full Access to Literacy for Including Information Books." *Language Arts* 68: 449–461.

Pilonieta, P. 2011. "The Expository Text Primer: A Teacher's Resource Guide for Using Expository Text." *New England Reading Association Journal* 46 (2): 45–51.

Rasinksi, T. 2014, April/May. "Delivering Supportive Fluency Instruction—Especially for Students Who Struggle." *Reading Today*, International Reading Association.

Repaskey, L., J. Schumm, and J. Johnson. 2017. "First and Fourth Grade Boys' and Girls' Preferences for and Perceptions About Narrative and Expository Text." *Reading Psychology* 38: 808–847.

Rosenblatt, L. 1978. *The Reader, the Text, the Poem: The Transactional Theory of the Literary Work*. Carbondale, IL: Southern Illinois University Press.

Shanahan, T. 2012, October 3. "Informational Text: Or How Thin Can You Slice the Salami?" Retrieved from https://shanahanonliteracy. com/blog/informational-text-or-how-thin-can-you-slice-the-salami.

Stead, T., and L. Hoyt. 2012. *Exploration in Nonfiction Writing, Grades K–5*. Portsmouth, NH: Heinemann.

Tuck, K. D., and D. R. Holmes. 2016. "Library/Media Centers in U.S. Public Schools: Growth, Staffing, and Resources." National Education Association. Retrieved from http://www.nea.org/home/67686.htm.

Chapter 4

Bober, T. 2019. Personal communication. June 4.

Clark, S. K., C. D. Jones, and D. R. Reutzel. 2013. "Using Text Structures of Information Books to Teach Writing in the Primary Grades." *Early Childhood Education Journal* 41: 265–271.

Diaz, A. 2019. Personal communication. June 6.

Dorfman, L., and R. Cappelli. 2009. *Nonfiction Mentor Texts: Teaching Informational Writing Through Children's Literature, K–8*. Portland, ME: Stenhouse.

Guthrie, J. T., A. L. Hoa, A. Wigfield, S. M. Tonks, N. M. Humenick, and E. Littles. 2007. "Reading Motivation and Reading Comprehension Growth in the Later Elementary Years." *Contemporary Educational Psychology* 32 (3): 282–313.

Kerper, R. M. 1998. "Choosing Quality Nonfiction Literature: Features for Accessing and Visualizing Information." In *Making Facts Come Alive: Choosing and Using Quality Nonfiction Literature K–9*, ed. R. A. Bamford and J. V. Kristo (55–74). 2nd ed. Norwood, MA: Christopher-Gordon.

Kiefer, B. Z. 2010. *Charlotte Huck's Children's Literature*. Boston: McGraw-Hill.

Lowery, R. M. 2019. Personal communication. June 17.

Miller, D., and S. Kelley. 2014. *Reading in the Wild: The Book Whisperer's Keys to Cultivating Lifelong Reading Habits*. San Francisco: Jossey-Bass.

Miller, D., and C. Sharp. 2018. *Game Changer! Book Access for All Kids*. New York: Scholastic.

Moss, B. 2003. *Exploring the Literature of Fact: Children's Nonfiction Trade Books in the Elementary Classroom*. New York: Guilford.

Picone, K. 2019. Personal communication. April 11.

Portalupi, J., and R. Fletcher. 2001. *Nonfiction Craft Lessons: Teaching Informational Writing K–8*. Portland, ME: Stenhouse.

Rosenblatt, L. 1999, March 14. "Louise Rosenblatt Interview." Department of Teaching and Learning, School of Education, University of Miami, Coral Gables, Florida. Retrieved from http://www.education.miami.edu/ep/rosenblatt/.

Stewart, M., and T. A. Young. 2018. "Defining and Describing Expository Literature." In *Does Nonfiction Equate Truth? Rethinking Disciplinary Boundaries Through Critical Literacies*, ed. V. Yenika-Agbaw, R. M. Lowery, and L. A. Hudock (11–24). Lanham, MD: Rowman and Littlefield.

Tovani, C. 2000. *I Read It! But I Don't Get It*. Portland, ME: Stenhouse.

Williams, J. P., A. M. Nubla-Kung, S. Pollini, K. B. Stafford, A. Garcia, and A. E. Snyder. 2007. "Teaching Cause-Effect Text Structure Through Social Studies Content to At-Risk Second Graders." *Journal of Learning Disabilities* 40: 111–120.

Chapter 5

Fang Z. 2006. "The Language Demands of Science Reading in Middle School." *International Journal of Science Education*. 28 (5): 491–520.

Keating, J. 2017. Personal communication. March 13.

Pike, K., and J. Mumper. 2004. *Making Nonfiction and Other Informational Texts Come Alive: A Practical Approach to Reading, Writing, and Using Nonfiction and Other Informational Texts Across the Curriculum*. New York: Pearson.

Pusey, A. 2018, February 3. "Getting to, I GET IT! Scaffolding in Nonfiction, Part 2." *Celebrate Science*. Retrieved from http://celebratescience.blogspot.com/2018/02/getting-to-i-get-it-scaffolding-in_3.html.

Stein, N. L., and C. G. Glenn. 1979. "Analysis of Story Comprehension in Elementary School Children." In *New Directions in Discourse Processing*, ed. R. O. Freedle (53–120). Norwood, NJ: Ablex.

Tovani, C. 2000. *I Read It! But I Don't Get It*. Portland, ME: Stenhouse.

Vincent, J. 2019. Personal communication. June 3.

Wheeler-Topen, J. 2019, January 15. "STEM Tuesday—Awesome Animal Antics—in the Classroom." From the Mixed-up Files of Middle Grade Authors. Retrieved from https://www.fromthemixedupfiles.com/2019/01/stem-tuesday-awesome-animal-antics-in-the-classroom/.

Chapter 6

Akhondi, M., F. A. Malayeri, and A. A. Samad. 2011. "How to Teach Expository Text Structure to Facilitate Reading Comprehension." *The Reading Teacher* 64: 368–372.

Bamford, R. A., and Kristo, J. V. 1998. "Choosing Quality Nonfiction Literature: Examining Aspects of Accuracy and Organization." In *Making Facts Come Alive: Choosing and Using Quality Nonfiction Literature K–9*, ed. R. Bamford and J. V. Kristo (19–38). 2nd ed. Norwood, MA: Christopher-Gordon.

Englert, C. C., and E. Hibert. 1984, February. "Children's Developing Awareness of Text Structures in Expository Material." *Journal of Educational Psychology* 76: 65–74.

Flood J., D. Lapp, and N. Farnan. 1986, February. "A Reading-Writing Procedure That Teaches Expository Paragraph Structure." *The Reading Teacher* 39: 556–562.

Guiberson, B. Z. 2017. Personal communication. March 13.

Jenkins, S. 2017. Personal communication. March 15.

Horowitz, R. 1985a, February. "Text Patterns: Part 1." *Journal of Reading* 28: 448–454.

———. 1985b. March. "Text Patterns: Part 2." *Journal of Reading* 28: 534–541.

McGee, L. M., and D. J. Richgels. 1985. April. "Teaching Expository Text Structure to Elementary Students." *The Reading Teacher* 28: 712–718.

Piccolo, J. 1987, May. "Expository Text Structure: Teaching and Learning Strategies." *The Reading Teacher* 40: 838–847.

Pike, K., and J. Mumper. 2004. *Making Nonfiction and Other Informational Texts Come Alive: A Practical Approach to Reading, Writing, and Using Nonfiction and Other Informational Texts Across the Curriculum*. New York: Pearson.

Short, K. G., and J. Armstrong. 1993. "Moving Toward Inquiry: Integrating Literature into the Science Curriculum." *The New Advocate* 6: 183–189.

Siu-Ruyan, Y. 1998. "Writing Nonfiction: Helping Students Teach Others What They Know." In *Making Facts Come Alive: Choosing and Using Quality Nonfiction Literature K–9*, ed. R. Bamford and J. V. Kristo (169–178). 2nd ed. Norwood, MA: Christopher-Gordon.

Chapter 7

Albee, S. 2017. Personal communication. March 9.

Englert, C. C., and E. Hibert. 1984. "Children's Developing Awareness of Text Structures in Expository Material." *Journal of Educational Psychology* 76: 65–74.

Fountas I., and G. Pinnell. 2016. *The Fountas and Pinnell Literacy Continuum*. Portsmouth, NH: Heinemann.

Guiberson, B. Z. 2017. Personal communication. March 13.

Levine, S. 2017. Personal communication. March 7.

Montgomery, H. 2018, October 8. "Nonfiction Authors Dig Deep by Heather L. Montgomery." *Celebrate Science*. Retrieved from http://celebratescience.blogspot.com/2018/10/nonfiction-authors-dig-deep-by-heather.html.

Moss, B. 2003. *Exploring the Literature of Fact: Children's Nonfiction Trade Books in the Elementary Classroom*. New York: Guilford.

National Governors Association Center for Best Practices and Council of Chief State School Officers (NGAC and CCSSO). 2010. *Common Core State Standards for English Language Arts and Literacy in History/Social Studies, Science, and Technical Subjects*. Washington, DC.

Park, L. S. 2019, February 10. "Just Do It." Society of Children's Book Writers and Illustrators Annual Winter Conference, New York.

Siu-Ruyan, Y. 1998. "Writing Nonfiction: Helping Students Teach Others What They Know." In *Making Facts Come Alive: Choosing and Using Quality Nonfiction Literature K–9*, ed. R. Bamford and J. V. Kristo (169–178). 2nd ed. Norwood, MA: Christopher-Gordon.

Vincent, J. 2019. Personal communication. June 3.

Chapter 8

Doiron, R. 2003. "Boy Books, Girl Books: Should We Reorganize Our School Library Collections?" *Teacher Librarian* 14–16.

Eurich, J. 2011, June 27. "Booktalks: The Great Equalizer in the Classroom." Lesley University Center for Reading Recovery and Literacy Collaborative. Retrieved from: https://lesleyuniversitycrrlc.wordpress.com/2011/06/27/book-talks-the-great-equalizer-in-theclassroom.

Gambrell, L. 1996. *Lively Discussions! Fostering Engaging Reading*. Newark, DE: International Literacy Association.

Guthrie, J.T., A. L. Hoa, A. Wigfield, S. M. Tonks, N. M. Humenick, and E. Littles. 2007. "Reading Motivation and Reading Comprehension Growth in the Later Elementary Years." *Contemporary Educational Psychology* 32 (3): 282–313.

Harvey, S., and A. Ward. 2017. *From Striving to Thriving: How to Grow Confident, Capable Readers.* New York: Scholastic.

Layne, S. 2009. *Igniting a Passion for Reading.* Portland, ME: Stenhouse.

Layne, S. L. 2015. *In Defense of Read-Aloud: Sustaining Best Practice.* Portland, ME: Stenhouse.

Mazzoni, S. A., and L. Gambrell. 1996. "Text Talk: Using Discussion to Promote Comprehension of Informational Texts." In *Lively Discussions: Fostering Engaged Reading*, ed. L. Gambrell and J. F. Almasi (134–148). Newark, DE: International Literacy Association.

Miller, D. 2009. *The Book Whisperer: Awakening the Inner Reader in Every Child.* San Francisco: Jossey-Bass.

Miller, D., and Kelley, S. 2014. *Reading in the Wild: The Book Whisperer's Keys to Cultivating Lifelong Reading Habits.* San Francisco: Jossey-Bass.

Repaskey, L., J. Schumm, and J. Johnson. 2017. "First and Fourth Grade Boys' and Girls' Preferences for and Perceptions About Narrative and Expository Text." *Reading Psychology* 38: 808–847.

Stead, T. 2014. "Nurturing the Inquiring Mind Through the Nonfiction Read-Aloud." *The Reading Teacher* 67 (7): 488–495.

Stewart, M. 2020, February 14. "March Madness Nonfiction." *Celebrate Science.* Retrieved from https://celebratescience.blogspot.com/2020/02/march-madness-nonfiction.html.

Vardell, S. 1998. "Using Read Aloud to Explore the Layers of Nonfiction." In *Making Facts Come Alive: Choosing and Using Quality Nonfiction Literature K–9*, ed. R. Bamford and J. V. Kristo (150–167). 2nd ed. Norwood, MA: Christopher-Gordon.

Yopp, R. H., and H. K. Yopp. 2006. "Information Texts as Read-Alouds at School and Home." *Journal of Literacy Research* 381: 37–51.

Zimmerman, S., and C. Hutchins, C. 2003. *7 Keys to Comprehension: How to Help Your Kids Read It and Get It!* New York: Three Rivers.

Chapter 9

Repaskey, L., J. Schumm, and J. Johnson. 2017. "First and Fourth Grade Boys' and Girls' Preferences for and Perceptions About Narrative and Expository Text." *Reading Psychology* 38: 808–847.

Springen, K. 2007. February 18. "Fourth-Grade Slump." *Newsweek*. Retrieved from https://www.newsweek.com/fourth -grade-slump-104873.

Young, T. 2019. Personal communication. December 6.

Book Cover Permissions

Chapter 1

Page 3: From SEA OTTER HEROES. Text copyright © 2017 by Patricia Newman. Reprinted with the permission of Millbrook Press, a division of Lerner Publishing Group, Inc. All rights reserved.

Pages 5 and 7: From WILDLIFE RANGER ACTION GUIDE: TRACK, SPOT & PROVIDE HEALTHY HABITAT FOR CREATURES CLOSE TO HOME. Text copyright © Mary Kay Carson. Published in 2020 by Storey Publishing. Cover used courtesy of Storey Publishing. All rights reserved.

Pages 5 and 7: From WE ARE GRATEFUL: OTSALIHELIGA. Text copyright © 2018 by Traci Sorell. Illustrations copyright © 2018 by Frané Lessac. Used with Permission by Charlesbridge Publishing.

Pages 5 and 7: From GOLDEN RETRIEVERS written by Sarah Frank. Copyright © 2019 by Lerner Publishing Group, Inc. Reprinted with the permission of Lerner Publications Company, a division of Lerner Publishing Group, Inc. All rights reserved.

Pages 5 and 6: From SPOOKED! HOW A RADIO BROADCAST AND THE WAR OF THE WORLDS SPARKED THE 1938 INVASION OF AMERICA. Text copyright © Gail Jarrow. Published in 2018 by Calkins Creek/Boyds Mills Press. Cover used by arrangement with Boyds Mills & Kane. All rights reserved.

Pages 5 and 6: From GAME CHANGERS: THE STORY OF VENUS AND SERENA WILLIAMS. Text copyright © Lesa Cline-Ransome. Illustrations copyright © James E. Ransome. Published in 2018 by Simon & Schuster. Cover used courtesy of Simon & Schuster Children's Publishing. All rights reserved.

Pages 5 and 6: From TWO BROTHERS, FOUR HANDS. Text copyright © Jan Greenberg and Sandra Jordan. Illustrations © Hadley Hooper. Published in 2019 by Holiday House. Cover used courtesy of Holiday House. All rights reserved.

Page 7: From RED-EYED TREE FROG. Text copyright @ 1999 Joy Cowley. Photographs copyright @ 1999 Nic Bishop. Reprinted with permission from Scholastic, Inc. All rights reserved.

Page 8: From FROG OR TOAD? HOW DO YOU KNOW? Text copyright © Melissa Stewart. Published in 2011 by Enslow Publishing. Cover used courtesy of Enslow Publishing, a Division of Rosen Publishing. All rights reserved.

Chapter 2

Pages 12 and 20: From WILDLIFE RANGER ACTION GUIDE: TRACK, SPOT & PROVIDE HEALTHY HABITAT FOR CREATURES CLOSE TO HOME. Text copyright © Mary Kay Carson. Published in 2020 by Storey Publishing. Cover used courtesy of Storey Publishing. All rights reserved.

Pages 12 and 15: From THE BOOK OF QUEENS: LEGENDARY LEADERS, FIERCE FEMALES, AND WONDER WOMEN WHO RULED THE WORLD. Text copyright © Stephanie Warren Drimmer. Published in 2019 by National Geographic. Cover used courtesy of National Geographic. All rights reserved.

Pages 12 and 14: From GOLDEN RETRIEVERS written by Sarah Frank. Copyright © 2019 by Lerner Publishing Group, Inc. Reprinted with the permission of Lerner Publications Company, a division of Lerner Publishing Group, Inc. All rights reserved.

Pages 12 and 18: From WE ARE GRATEFUL: OTSALIHELIGA. Text copyright © 2018 by Traci Sorell. Illustrations copyright © 2018 by Frané Lessac. Used with Permission by Charlesbridge Publishing.

Pages 12 and 16: From TWO BROTHERS, FOUR HANDS. Text copyright © Jan Greenberg and Sandra Jordan. Illustrations © Hadley Hooper. Published in 2019 by Holiday House. Cover used courtesy of Holiday House. All rights reserved.

Page 14: From CORAL REEFS. Text and illustrations copyright © Gail Gibbons. Published in 2019 by Holiday House. Cover used courtesy of Holiday House. All rights reserved.

Page 14: From MONSTER TRUCKS. Written by Matt Doeden. Published in 2018 by Capstone Publishing. Cover used courtesy of Capstone Publishing. All rights reserved.

Page 14: From ABOUT HABITATS: RIVERS AND STREAMS. Text copyright © 2019 by Cathryn Sill. Illustrations copyright © 2019 by John Sill. Published by arrangement with Peachtree Publishing Company Inc. All rights reserved.

Page 15: From EYE SPY: WILD WAYS ANIMALS SEE THE WORLD. Text copyright © Guillaume Duprat. Published in 2018 by What on Earth Books. Cover used courtesy of What on Earth Books. All rights reserved.

Page 15: From NORTH AMERICA: A FOLD-OUT GRAPHIC HISTORY. Text copyright © Sarah Albee. Published in 2019 by What on Earth Books. Cover used courtesy of What on Earth Books. All rights reserved.

Page 15: From OCEAN: SECRETS OF THE DEEP. Text copyright © Sabrina Weiss and Giulia De Amicis. Published in 2019 by What on Earth Books. Cover used courtesy of What on Earth Books. All rights reserved.

Page 16: From JOAN PROCTOR, REPTILE DOCTOR: THE WOMAN WHO LOVED REPTILES. New York: Knopf, 2018. Valdez, Patricia. Text copyright © 2018 Patricia Valdez. Illustrations copyright © 2018 Felicita Sala. Published in 2018 by Knopf, a division of Penguin Random House LLC. Cover used courtesy of Penguin Random House LLC. All rights reserved.

Page 16: From KARL'S NEW BEAK. Text copyright © Lela Nargi. Published in 2019 by Capstone. Cover used courtesy of Capstone. All rights reserved.

Page 16: From YOU'RE INVITED TO A MOTH BALL: A NIGHTTIME INSECT CELEBRATION. Text copyright © 2020 by Loree Griffin Burns. Photographs copyright © 2020 by Ellen Harasimowicz. Used with Permission by Charlesbridge Publishing.

Page 18: From A BUTTERFLY IS PATIENT. Text copyright © 2011 by Diana Hutts Aston. Illustrations copyright © 2011 by Sylvia Long. Used with the permission of Chronicle Books LLC, San Francisco. All rights reserved.

Page 18: From ROTTEN: VULTURES, BEETLES, SLIME AND NATURE'S OTHER DECOMPOSERS. Text copyright © Anita Sanchez. Published in 2019 by Houghton Mifflin Harcourt. Cover used courtesy of Houghton Mifflin Harcourt. All rights reserved.

Page 18: From WHAT IF YOU HAD T. REX TEETH? AND OTHER DINOSAUR PARTS. Text copyright © 2019 Sandra Markle. Illustrations © 2019 Howard McWilliam. Reprinted with permission from Scholastic, Inc. All rights reserved.

Page 18: From WOMEN IN ART: 50 FEARLESS CREATIVES WHO INSPIRED THE WORLD © Rachel Ignotofsky. Published in 2018 by Ten Speed Press, a division of Penguin Random House LLC. Cover used courtesy of Penguin Random House LLC. All rights reserved.

Page 20: From CODE THIS! PUZZLES, GAMES, CHALLENGES, AND COMPUTER CODING CONCEPTS FOR THE PROBLEM SOLVER IN YOU. Text copyright © Jennifer Szymanski. Published in 2019 by National Geographic. Cover used courtesy of National Geographic. All rights reserved.

Page 20: From COOKING CLASS GLOBAL FEAST! 44 RECIPES THAT CELEBRATE THE WORLD'S CULTURES. Text copyright © Deanna F.

Cook. Published in 2019 by Storey Publishing. Cover used courtesy of Storey Publishing.

Page 20: From RALPH MASIELLO'S ALIEN DRAWING BOOK. Text copyright © 2019 by Ralph Masiello. Used with Permission by Charlesbridge Publishing.

Page 21: From SNIFFER DOGS: HOW DOGS (AND THEIR NOSES) SAVE THE WORLD. Text copyright © Nancy Castaldo. Published in 2014 by Houghton Mifflin Harcourt. Cover used courtesy of Houghton Mifflin Harcourt.

Pages 21: From SPOOKED! HOW A RADIO BROADCAST AND THE WAR OF THE WORLDS SPARKED THE 1938 INVASION OF AMERICA. Text copyright © Gail Jarrow. Published in 2018 by Calkins Creek/Boyds Mills Press. Cover used by arrangement with Boyds Mills & Kane.

Chapter 3

Page 22: From PIPSQUEAKS, SLOWPOKES, AND STINKERS. Text copyright © 2018 by Melissa Stewart. Illustrations copyright © 2018 by Stephanie Laberis. Interior spread published by arrangement with Peachtree Publishing Company Inc.

Page 26: From WHAT IF YOU HAD T. REX TEETH? AND OTHER DINOSAUR PARTS. Text copyright © 2019 Sandra Markle. Illustrations © 2019 Howard McWilliam. Reprinted with permission from Scholastic, Inc.

Page 29: From CAN AN AARDVARK BARK?. Text copyright © Melissa Stewart. Illustrations © Steve Jenkins. Published in 2017 by Beach Lane Books/Simon & Schuster. Cover used courtesy of Simon & Schuster Children's Publishing.

Page 35: From BOY, WERE WE WRONG ABOUT DINOSAURS. Text copyright © 2008 Kathleen Kudlinski. Illustrations copyright © 2008 S. D. Schindler. Published in 2008 by Dutton, a division of Penguin Random House LLC. Cover used courtesy of Penguin Random House LLC.

Chapter 4

Page 39: From THIS IS HOW WE DO IT. Text and illustrations copyright © 2017 by Matt LaMothe. Used with the permission of Chronicle Books LLC, San Francisco.

Page 44: From BENJAMIN FRANKLIN, AMERICAN GENIUS: HIS LIFE AND IDEAS WITH 21 ACTIVITIES. Text copyright © Brandon Marie Miller. Published in 2009 by Chicago Review Press. Cover used courtesy of Chicago Review Press. All rights reserved.

Page 45: From NOW & BEN: THE MODERN INVENTIONS OF BENJAMIN FRANKLIN. Copyright © 2006 by Gene Barretta. Reprinted with permission from Henry Holt Books for Young Readers. ALL RIGHTS RESERVED.

Page 46: From WEATHER. Text copyright © 2006 Seymour Simon. Reprinted with permission from HarperCollins Books for Young Readers. All rights reserved.

Page 46: From ULTIMATE WEATHER-PEDIA. Text copyright © Stephanie Warren Drimmer. Published in 2019 by National Geographic. Cover used courtesy of National Geographic. All rights reserved.

Page 52: From WAIT, REST, PAUSE: DORMANCY IN NATURE. Text copyright © 2019 by Marcie Flinchum Atkins. Reprinted with the pemission of Millbrook Press, a division of Lerner Publishing Group, Inc. All rights reserved.

Page 55: From TINY CREATURES. Text copyright © 2014 by Nicola Davies. Illustrations copyright © 2014 by Emily Sutton. Reproduced by permission of the publisher, Candlewick Press, Somerville, MA on behalf of Walker Books, London.

Page 60: From WEEDS FIND A WAY. Text copyright © Cindy Jenson-Elliott. Illustrations © Carolyn Fisher. Published in 2014 by Beach Lane Books/Simon & Schuster. Cover used courtesy of Simon & Schuster Children's Publishing. All rights reserved.

Chapter 5

Page 61: From MANY. Text copyright © 2017 by Nicola Davies. Illustrations copyright © 2017 by Emily Sutton. Reproduced by permission of the publisher, Candlewick Press, Somerville, MA on behalf of Walker Books, London.

Page 62: From WHAT DO YOU DO WITH A TAIL LIKE THIS? Text copyright © Steve Jenkins and Robin Page. Published in 2003 by Houghton Mifflin Harcourt. Interior spread used courtesy of Houghton Mifflin Harcourt. All rights reserved.

Page 64: From ZOOM IN ON BEES. Text copyright © Melissa Stewart. Published in 2014 by Enslow Publishing. Cover used courtesy of Enslow Publishing, a division of Rosen Publishing. All rights reserved.

Page 65: From ICK! DELIGHTFULLY DISGUSTING ANIMAL DINNERS, DWELLINGS, AND DEFENSES. Text copyright © Melissa Stewart. Published in 2020 by National Geographic. Cover and interior spread used courtesy of National Geographic. All rights reserved.

Page 67: From GIANT SQUID. Text copyright © 2016 by Candace Fleming. Illustrations © 2016 by Eric Rohman. Reprinted with permission from Roaring Brook Press, a division of Holtzbrinck Publishing Holdings Limited Partnership. ALL RIGHTS RESERVED.

Pages 69 and 71: From MAMA BUILT A LITTLE NEST. Text copyright © 2014 Jennifer Ward. Illustrations © 2014 Steve Jenkins. Published in 2014 by Beach Lane Books/Simon & Schuster. Cover used courtesy of Simon & Schuster Children's Publishing. All rights reserved.

Pages 69 and 72: From AN EGG IS QUIET. Text copyright © 2006 by Diana Hutts Aston. Illustrations copyright © 2006 by Sylvia Long. Used with the pemission of Chronicle Books LLC, San Francisco. All rights reserved.

Page 69: From PINK IS FOR BLOBFISH: DISCOVERING THE WORLD'S PERFECTLY PINK ANIMALS. Text copyright © 2016 Jess Keating. Illustrations copyright © 2016 David deGrand. Published in 2016 by Knopf, a division of Penguin Random House LLC. Cover used courtesy of Penguin Random House LLC. All rights reserved.

Pages 70 and 72: From HOW TO CLEAN A HIPPOPOTAMUS: A LOOK AT UNUSUAL ANIMAL PARTNERSHIPS. Text copyright © Steve Jenkins and Robin Page. Published in 2010 by Houghton Mifflin Harcourt. Cover and interior used courtesy of Houghton Mifflin Harcourt. All rights reserved.

Page 71: From MOVE! Text and illustrations copyright © Steve Jenkins and Robin Page. Published in 2006 by Houghton Mifflin Harcourt. Cover used courtesy of Houghton Mifflin Harcourt. All rights reserved.

Page 71: From WHERE IN THE WILD? CAMOUFLAGED CREATURES CONCEALED . . . AND REVEALED. Text copyright © David M. Schwartz and Yael Schy. Photographs copyright © Dwight Kuhn. Published in 2011 by

Tricycle Press, a division of Penguin Random House LLC. Cover used courtesy of Penguin Random House LLC. All rights reserved.

Page 73: From SNOWY OWL INVASION!: TRACKING AN UNUSUAL MIGRATION. Text copyright © 2018 by Sandra Markle. Reprinted with the permission of Millbrook Press, a division of Lerner Publishing Group, Inc. All rights reserved.

Page 73: From ITCH! EVERYTHING YOU DIDN'T WANT TO KNOW ABOUT WHAT MAKES YOU SCRATCH. Text copyright © Anita Sanchez. Illustrations copyright © Gilbert Ford. Published in 2018 by Houghton Mifflin Harcourt. Cover used courtesy of Houghton Mifflin Harcourt. All rights reserved.

Page 74: From DEATH EATERS: MEET NATURE'S SCAVENGERS. Text copyright © 2019 by Kelly Milner Halls. Reprinted with the permission of Millbrook Press, a division of Lerner Publishing Group, Inc. All rights reserved.

Page 75: From SUPER GEAR: NANOTECHNOLOGY AND SPORTS TEAM UP. Text copyright © 2016 by Jennifer Swanson. Images copyright © by individual copyright holders. Used with Permission by Charlesbridge Publishing.

Page 76: From HEDY LAMARR'S DOUBLE LIFE: HOLLYWOOD LEGEND AND BRILLIANT INVENTOR by Laurie Wallmark. Illustrated by Kathy Wu. Published in 2019 by Sterling Children's Books. Cover used courtesy of Sterling Publishing Co., Inc. All rights reserved.

Page 76: From MARIO AND THE HOLE IN THE SKY HOW A CHEMIST SAVED OUR PLANET. Text copyright © 2019 by Elizabeth Rusch. Illustrations copyright © 2019 by Teresa Martínez. Used with Permission by Charlesbridge Publishing.

Chapter 6

Page 78: From DID YOU BURP? HOW TO ASK QUESTIONS . . . OR NOT! Text copyright © 2019 by April Pulley Sayre. Illustrations copyright © 2019 by Leeza Hernandez. Used with Permission by Charlesbridge Publishing.

Page 79: From MANY. Text copyright © 2017 by Nicola Davies. Illustrations copyright © 2017 by Emily Sutton. Reproduced by permission of the publisher, Candlewick Press, Somerville, MA on behalf of Walker Books, London.

Page 79: From THE FROG BOOK. Text copyright © Steve Jenkins. Published in 2019 by Houghton Mifflin Harcourt. Cover used courtesy of Houghton Mifflin Harcourt. All rights reserved.

Page 79: From BUGGED: HOW INSECTS CHANGED HISTORY. Text copyright © Sarah Albee. Published in 2014 by Bloomsbury. Cover used courtesy of Bloomsbury. All rights reserved.

Page 79: From HOW TO SWALLOW A PIG: STEP-BY-STEP ADVICE FROM THE ANIMAL KINGDOM. Text copyright © Steve Jenkins and Robin Page. Published in 2015 by Houghton Mifflin Harcourt. Cover used courtesy of Houghton Mifflin Harcourt. All rights reserved.

Pages 80 and 87: From RODENT RASCALS. Text and illustration copyright © Roxie Munro. Published in 2018 by Holiday House. Cover used courtesy of Holiday House. All rights reserved.

Page 80: From DAYLIGHT STARLIGHT WILDLIFE. Text and illustration copyright © Wendell Minor. Published in 2005 by Nancy Paulsen Books, a division of Penguin Random House LLC. Cover used courtesy of Penguin Random House LLC. All rights reserved.

Pages 80 and 89: From NEVER SMILE AT A MONKEY: AND 17 OTHER IMPORTANT THINGS TO REMEMBER. Text copyright © Steve Jenkins. Published in 2014 by Houghton Mifflin Harcourt. Cover used courtesy of Houghton Mifflin Harcourt. All rights reserved.

Page 80: From IF SHARKS DISAPPEARED. Text copyright © 2017 by Lily Williams. Reprinted with permission from Roaring Brook Press, a division of Holtzbrinck Publishing Holdings Limited Partnership. ALL RIGHTS RESERVED.

Page 80: From BOY, WERE WE WRONG ABOUT DINOSAURS. Text copyright © 2008 Kathleen Kudlinski. Illustrations copyright © 2008 S. D. Schindler. Published in 2008 by Dutton, a division of Penguin Random House LLC. Cover used courtesy of Penguin Random House LLC. All rights reserved.

Page 80: From SHE PERSISTED: 13 AMERICAN WOMEN WHO CHANGED THE WORLD. Text copyright © 2017 Chelsea Clinton. Illustrations copyright © 2017 Alexandra Boiger. Published in 2017 by Philomel, a division of Penguin Random House LLC. Cover used courtesy of Penguin Random House LLC. All rights reserved.

Page 81: From HOMES IN THE WILD: WHERE BABY MAMMALS AND THEIR PARENTS LIVE. Text and illustrations copyright © 2019 by Lita Judge. Reprinted with permission from Roaring Brook Press, a division of Holtzbrinck Publishing Holdings Limited Partnership. All rights reserved.

Page 81: From PINK IS FOR BLOBFISH: DISCOVERING THE WORLD'S PERFECTLY PINK ANIMALS. Text copyright © 2016 Jess Keating. Illustrations copyright © 2016 David deGrand. Published in 2016 by Knopf, a division of Penguin Random House LLC. Cover used courtesy of Penguin Random House LLC. All rights reserved.

Page 82: From HATCH! by Roxie Munro, published in the United States by Two Lions, 2011. Text and illustrations copyright © 2011 by Roxie Munro. Reprinted with permission of Amazon Publishing, www.apub.com, all rights reserved.

Page 82: From DO SHARKS GLOW IN THE DARK? . . . AND OTHER SHARK-TASTIC QUESTIONS by Mary Kay Carson. Published in 2019 by Sterling Children's Books. Cover used courtesy of Sterling Publishing Co., Inc. All rights reserved.

Page 83: From BIRDS OF A FEATHER: BOWERBIRDS AND ME. Text and illustrations copyright Susan L. Roth. Published in 2019 by Holiday House. Cover used courtesy of Holiday House. All rights reserved.

Page 83: From IF YOU HOPPED LIKE A FROG. Text copyright © 1999 David M. Schwartz. Illustrations © 1999 James Warhola. Reprinted with permission from Scholastic, Inc. All rights reserved.

Page 85: From RED-EYED TREE FROG. Text copyright @ 1999 Joy Cowley. Photographs copyright @ 1999 Nic Bishop. Reprinted with permission from Scholastic, Inc. All rights reserved.

Page 85: From FROG SONG. Text copyright © 2013 by Brenda Guiberson. Illustrations © 2013 by Gennady Spirin. Reprinted with permission from Henry Holt Books for Young Readers. ALL RIGHTS RESERVED.

Page 85: From THE HIDDEN LIFE OF A TOAD. Text and photographs copyright © 2017 by Doug Wechsler. Used with Permission by Charlesbridge Publishing.

Page 85: From A PLACE FOR FROGS. Text copyright © 2009, 2016 by Melissa Stewart. Illustrations copyright © 2009, 2016 by Higgins Bond. Published by arrangement with Peachtree Publishing Company Inc. All rights reserved.

Page 86: From SWIRL BY SWIRL: SPIRALS IN NATURE. Text copyright © Joyce Sidman. Published in 2011 by Houghton Mifflin Harcourt. Cover used courtesy of Houghton Mifflin Harcourt. All rights reserved.

Page 87: From THE NEXT PRESIDENT: THE UNEXPECTED BEGINNINGS AND UNWRITTEN FUTURE OF AMERICA'S PRESIDENTS. Text copyright © 2020 Kate Messner. Illustrations copyright © 2020 Adam Rex. Used with the permission of Chronicle Books LLC, San Francisco. All rights reserved.

Page 87: From LINCOLN AND KENNEDY: A PAIR TO COMPARE. Text and illustrations copyright © 2016 by Gene Barretta. Reprinted with permission from Henry Holt Books for Young Readers. ALL RIGHTS RESERVED.

Page 88: From CAN AN AARDVARK BARK?. Text copyright © Melissa Stewart. Illustrations © Steve Jenkins. Published in 2017 by Beach Lane Books/Simon & Schuster. Cover used courtesy of Simon & Schuster Children's Publishing. All rights reserved.

Page 90: From EARTH: FEELING THE HEAT. Text copyright © 2010 by Brenda Guiberson. Illustrations © 2010 by Chad Wallace. Reprinted with permission from Henry Holt Books for Young Readers. ALL RIGHTS RESERVED.

Page 90: From FEATHERED DINOSAURS. Text copyright © 2016 by Brenda Guiberson. Illustrations © 2016 by William Low. Reprinted with permission from Henry Holt Books for Young Readers. ALL RIGHTS RESERVED.

Pages 90 and 92: From WHAT DO YOU DO WITH A TAIL LIKE THIS? Text copyright © Steve Jenkins and Robin Page. Published in 2003 by Houghton Mifflin Harcourt. Cover used courtesy of Houghton Mifflin Harcourt. All rights reserved.

Chapter 7

Page 96: From GOLDEN RETRIEVERS written by Sarah Frank. Copyright © 2019 by Lerner Publishing Group, Inc. Reprinted with the permission of Lerner Publications Company, a division of Lerner Publishing Group, Inc. All rights reserved.

Page 96: From TWO BROTHERS, FOUR HANDS. Text copyright © Jan Greenberg and Sandra Jordan. Illustrations © Hadley Hooper. Published in 2019 by Holiday House. Cover used courtesy of Holiday House. All rights reserved.

Page 96: From WILDLIFE RANGER ACTION GUIDE: TRACK, SPOT & PROVIDE HEALTHY HABITAT FOR CREATURES CLOSE TO HOME. Text copyright © Mary Kay Carson. Published in 2020 by Storey Publishing. Cover used courtesy of Storey Publishing. All rights reserved.

Page 96: From THE BOOK OF QUEENS: LEGENDARY LEADERS, FIERCE FEMALES, AND WONDER WOMEN WHO RULED THE WORLD. Text copyright © Stephanie Warren Drimmer. Published in 2019 by National Geographic. Cover used courtesy of National Geographic. All rights reserved.

Page 96: From WE ARE GRATEFUL: OTSALIHELIGA. Text copyright © 2018 by Traci Sorell. Illustrations copyright © 2018 by Frané Lessac. Used with Permission by Charlesbridge Publishing.

Page 97: From MONSTER TRUCKS. Written by Matt Doeden. Published in 2018 by Capstone. Cover used courtesy of Capstone. All rights reserved.

Page 99: From NORTH AMERICA: A FOLD-OUT GRAPHIC HISTORY. Text copyright © Sarah Albee. Published in 2019 by What on Earth Books. Cover used courtesy of What on Earth Books. All rights reserved.

Page 100: From ITCH! EVERYTHING YOU DIDN'T WANT TO KNOW ABOUT WHAT MAKES YOU SCRATCH. Text copyright © Anita Sanchez. Illustrations copyright © Gilbert Ford. Published in 2018 by Houghton Mifflin Harcourt. Cover used courtesy of Houghton Mifflin Harcourt. All rights reserved.

Pages 101 and 105: From GIANT SQUID Text copyright © 2016 by Candace Fleming. Illustrations copyright © 2016 by Eric Rohman. Reprinted with permission from Roaring Brook Press, a division of Holtzbrinck Publishing Holdings Limited Partnership. ALL RIGHTS RESERVED.

Page 102: From PINK IS FOR BLOBFISH: DISCOVERING THE WORLD'S PERFECTLY PINK ANIMALS. Text copyright © 2016 Jess Keating. Illustrations copyright © 2016 David deGrand. Published in 2016 by Knopf, a division of Penguin Random House LLC. Cover used courtesy of Penguin Random House LLC. All rights reserved.

Page 102: From A BUTTERFLY IS PATIENT. Text copyright © 2011 by Diana Hutts Aston. Illustrations copyright © 2011 by Sylvia Long. Used with the permission of Chronicle Books LLC, San Francisco. All rights reserved.

Page 103: From WE ARE GRATEFUL: OTSALIHELIGA. Text copyright © 2018 by Traci Sorell. Illustrations copyright © 2018 by Frané Lessac. Used with Permission by Charlesbridge Publishing.

Page 104: From FROG SONG. Text copyright © 2013 by Brenda Guiberson. Illustrations © 2013 by Gennady Spirin. Reprinted with permission from Henry Holt Books for Young Readers. ALL RIGHTS RESERVED.

Page 104: From POISON: DEADLY DEEDS, PERILOUS PROFESSIONS, AND MURDEROUS MEDICINES. Text copyright © 2017 Sarah Albee. Published in 2016 by Crown, a division of Penguin Random House LLC. Cover used courtesy of Penguin Random House LLC. All rights reserved.

Page 105: From BEFORE SHE WAS HARRIET: THE STORY OF HARRIET TUBMAN. Text copyright © Lesa-Cline Ransome. Illustrations © James E. Ransome. Published in 2017 by Holiday House. Cover used courtesy of Holiday House. All rights reserved.

Page 105: From IF YOU FIND A ROCK. Text copyright © Peggy Christian. Published in 2000 by Houghton Mifflin Harcourt. Cover used courtesy of Houghton Mifflin Harcourt. All rights reserved.

Page 105: From PLANTING THE WILD GARDEN. Text copyright © 2011 by Kathryn O. Galbraith. Illustrations copyright © 2011 by Wendy Anderson Halperin. Published by arrangement with Peachtree Publishing Company Inc. All rights reserved.

Page 107: From TINY CREATURES. Text copyright © 2014 by Nicola Davies. Illustrations copyright © 2014 by Emily Sutton. Reproduced by permission of the publisher, Candlewick Press, Somerville, MA, on behalf of Walker Books, London.

Page 107: From BONE BY BONE: COMPARING ANIMAL SKELETONS. Text copyright © 2014 by Sara Levine. Illustrations copyright © 2014 by T. S. Spookytooth. Reprinted with the permission of Millbrook Press, a division of Lerner Publishing Group, Inc. All rights reserved.

Pages 108 and 111: From FLYING DEEP: CLIMB INSIDE DEEP-SEA SUBMERSIBLE ALVIN. Text copyright © 2018 by Michelle Cusolito. Illustrations copyright © 2018 by Nicole Wong. Used with Permission by Charlesbridge Publishing.

Page 111: From IF YOU HOPPED LIKE A FROG. Text copyright © 1999 David M. Schwartz. Illustrations © 1999 James Warhola. Reprinted with permission from Scholastic, Inc. All rights reserved.

Pages 111 and 112: From POET: THE REMARKABLE STORY OF GEORGE MOSES HORTON. Text copyright © 2015 by Don Tate. Illustrations copyright © 2015 by Don Tate. Published by arrangement with Peachtree Publishing Company Inc. All rights reserved.

Page 111: From THIS IS HOW WE DO IT. Text and illustrations copyright © 2017 by Matt LaMothe. Used with the permission of Chronicle Books LLC, San Francisco. All rights reserved.

Page 116: From THE DEADLIEST CREATURE IN THE WORLD. Text copyright © 2016 by Brenda Guiberson; Illustrations © 2016 by Gennady Spirin. Reprinted with permission from Henry Holt Books for Young Readers. ALL RIGHTS RESERVED.

Page 116: From SUN! ONE IN A BILLION. Text copyright © 2018 by Stacey McAnulty. Illustrations © 2018 by Christian Robinson. Reprinted with permission from Roaring Brook Press, a division of Holtzbrinck Publishing Holdings Limited Partnership. ALL RIGHTS RESERVED.

Chapter 8

Page 117: From BORN IN THE WILD: BABY MAMMALS AND THEIR PARENTS. Text and illustrations copyright © 2014 by Lita Judge. Reprinted with permission from Roaring Brook Press, a division of Holtzbrinck Publishing Holdings Limited Partnership. ALL RIGHTS RESERVED.

Pages 118 and 128: From CUTE AS AN AXOLOTL: DISCOVERING THE WORLD'S MOST ADORABLE ANIMALS. Text copyright © 2019 Jess Keating. Illustrations copyright © 2019 David deGrand. Published in 2016 by Knopf, a division of Penguin Random House LLC. Cover used courtesy of Penguin Random House LLC. All rights reserved.

Page 119: From FIRST DAY JITTERS. Text copyright © 2000 by Julie Danneberg. Illustrations copyright © 2000 by Judy Love. Used with Permission by Charlesbridge Publishing.

Page 126: From AN EGG IS QUIET. Text copyright © 2006 by Diana Hutts Aston. Illustrations copyright © 2006 by Sylvia Long. Used with the permission of Chronicle Books LLC, San Francisco. All rights reserved.

Pages 126 and 134: From BIRDS OF A FEATHER: BOWERBIRDS AND ME. Text copyright © Susan Roth. Published in 2019 by Holiday House. Cover used courtesy of Holiday House. All rights reserved.

Page 127: From PIPSQUEAKS, SLOWPOKES, AND STINKERS: CELEBRATING ANIMAL UNDERDOGS. Text copyright © 2018 by Melissa Stewart. Illustrations copyright © 2018 by Stephanie Laberis. Published by arrangement with Peachtree Publishing Company Inc. All rights reserved.

Page 127: From FLYING FROGS AND WALKING FISH: LEAPING LEMURS, TUMBLING TOADS, JET-PROPELLED JELLYFISH, AND MORE SURPRISING WAYS THAT ANIMALS MOVE. Text copyright © Steve Jenkins and Robin Page. Published in 2016 by Houghton Mifflin Harcourt. Cover used courtesy of Houghton Mifflin Harcourt. All rights reserved.

Page 128: From WARBLER WAVE. Text and photographs copyright © 2018 April Pulley Sayre. Published in 2018 by Beach Lane Books/Simon & Schuster. Cover used courtesy of Simon & Schuster Children's Publishing. All rights reserved.

Page 128: From HOW TO SWALLOW A PIG: STEP-BY-STEP ADVICE FROM THE ANIMAL KINGDOM. Text copyright © Steve Jenkins and Robin Page. Published in 2015 by Houghton Mifflin Harcourt. Cover used courtesy of Houghton Mifflin Harcourt. All rights reserved.

Page 130: From BEFORE SHE WAS HARRIET: THE STORY OF HARRIET TUBMAN. Text copyright © Lesa-Cline Ransome. Illustrations © James E. Ransome. Published in 2017 by Holiday House. Cover used courtesy of Holiday House. All rights reserved.

Page 130: From GAME CHANGERS: THE STORY OF VENUS AND SERENA WILLIAMS. Text copyright © Lesa Cline-Ransome. Illustrations copyright © James E. Ransome. Published in 2018 by Simon & Schuster. Cover used courtesy of Simon & Schuster Children's Publishing. All rights reserved.

Page 130: From SHE PERSISTED: 13 AMERICAN WOMEN WHO CHANGED THE WORLD. Text copyright © 2017 Chelsea Clinton. Illustrations copyright © 2017 Alexandra Boiger. Published in 2017 by

Philomel, a division of Penguin Random House LLC. Cover used courtesy of Penguin Random House LLC. All rights reserved.

Page 133: From DEATH EATERS: MEET NATURE'S SCAVENGERS. Text copyright © 2019 by Kelly Milner Halls. Reprinted with the permission of Millbrook Press, a division of Lerner Publishing Group, Inc. All rights reserved.

Page 133: From ROTTEN: VULTURES, BEETLES, SLIME AND NATURE'S OTHER DECOMPOSERS. Text copyright © Anita Sanchez. Illustrations copyright © Gilbert Ford. Published in 2019 by Houghton Mifflin Harcourt. Cover used courtesy of Houghton Mifflin Harcourt. All rights reserved.

Page 133: From DOG DAYS OF HISTORY: THE INCREDIBLE STORY OF OUR BEST FRIENDS. Text copyright © Sarah Albee. Published in 2018 by National Geographic. Cover used courtesy of National Geographic. All rights reserved.

Page 133: From MADE FOR EACH OTHER: WHY DOGS AND PEOPLE ARE THE PERFECT PARTNERS. Text copyright © 2018 Dorothy Hinshaw Patent. Published in 2018 by Crown, a division of Penguin Random House LLC. Cover used courtesy of Penguin Random House LLC. All rights reserved.

Page 133: From EYE SPY: WILD WAYS ANIMALS SEE THE WORLD. Text copyright © Guillaume Duprat. Published in 2018 by What on Earth Books. Cover used courtesy of What on Earth Books. All rights reserved.

Page 133: From WHAT IF YOU HAD ANIMAL EYES? Text copyright © 2017 Sandra Markle. Illustrations © 2017 Howard McWilliam. Reprinted with permission from Scholastic, Inc. All rights reserved.

Page 133: From FLYING DEEP: CLIMB INSIDE DEEP-SEA SUBMERSIBLE ALVIN. Text copyright © 2018 by Michelle Cusolito. Illustrations copyright © 2018 by Nicole Wong. Used with Permission by Charlesbridge Publishing.

Page 133: From OTIS AND WILL DISCOVER THE DEEP. Text copyright © Barbara Rosenstock and Katherine Roy. Published in 2018 by Little Brown Hachette. Cover used courtesy of Little Brown Hachette. All rights reserved.

Page 133: From SEEDS MOVE. Text and photographs copyright © 2019 Robin Page. Published in 2019 by Beach Lane Books/Simon & Schuster. Cover used courtesy of Simon & Schuster Children's Publishing. All rights reserved.

Page 133: From A SEED IS THE START. Text copyright © Melissa Stewart. Published in 2018 by National Geographic. Cover used courtesy of National Geographic. All rights reserved.

Chapter 9

Pages 137, 140, and 143: From GIANT SQUID. Text copyright © 2016 by Candace Fleming. Illustrations © 2016 by Eric Rohman. Reprinted with permission from Roaring Brook Press, a division of Holtzbrinck Publishing Holdings Limited Partnership. ALL RIGHTS RESERVED.

Pages 137 and 140: From HOW TO BE AN ELEPHANT. Text copyright © 2017 by Katherine Roy. Reprinted with permission from Roaring Brook Press, a division of Holtzbrinck Publishing Holdings Limited Partnership. ALL RIGHTS RESERVED.

Pages 137 and 142: From NEIGHBORHOOD SHARKS: HUNTING WITH THE GREAT WHITES OF CALIFORNIA'S FARALLON ISLANDS. Text copyright © 2014 by Katherine Roy. Reprinted with permission from Roaring Brook Press, a division of Holtzbrinck Publishing Holdings Limited Partnership. ALL RIGHTS RESERVED.

Page 139: From BIRDS OF A FEATHER: BOWERBIRDS AND ME. Text copyright © Susan Roth. Published in 2019 by Holiday House. Cover used courtesy of Holiday House. All rights reserved.

Page 139: From THE IMPORTANT THING ABOUT MARGARET WISE BROWN. Text copyright © 2019 Mac Barnett. Illustrations copyright © 2019 Sarah Jacoby. Reprinted with permission from Balzer + Bray, a division of HarperCollins Books for Young Readers. All rights reserved.

Page 140: From MASTERS OF DISGUISE: AMAZING ANIMAL TRICKSTERS. Text copyright © 2016 by Rebecca L. Johnson. Reprinted with the permission of Millbrook Press, a division of Lerner Publishing Group, Inc. All rights reserved.

Pages 140 and 142: From SNIFFER DOGS: HOW DOGS (AND THEIR NOSES) SAVE THE WORLD. Text copyright © Nancy Castaldo. Published in 2014 by Houghton Mifflin Harcourt. Cover used courtesy of Houghton Mifflin Harcourt. All rights reserved.

Page 142: From THE GREAT MONKEY RESCUE: SAVING THE GOLDEN LION TAMARINS. Text copyright © 2018 by Sandra Markle. Reprinted with the permission of Millbrook Press, a division of Lerner Publishing Group, Inc. All rights reserved.

Page 142: From SNOWY OWL INVASION!. Text copyright © 2018 by Sandra Markle. Reprinted with the permission of Millbrook Press, a division of Lerner Publishing Group, Inc. All rights reserved.

Pages 142: From ZOMBIE MAKERS: TRUE STORIES OF NATURE'S UNDEAD. Text copyright © 2013 by Rebecca L. Johnson. Reprinted with the permission of Millbrook Press, a division of Lerner Publishing Group, Inc. All rights reserved.

Appendix E

Page 157: From ACTUAL SIZE. Text and illustrations copyright © Steve Jenkins. Published in 2014 by Houghton Mifflin Harcourt. Cover used courtesy of Houghton Mifflin Harcourt. All rights reserved.

Page 157: From BECAUSE OF AN ACORN. Text copyright © 2016 Lola M. Schaefer. Illustrations copyright © 2016 Adam Schaefer. Used with the permission of Chronicle Books LLC, San Francisco. All rights reserved.

Page 157: From BORN IN THE WILD: BABY MAMMALS AND THEIR PARENTS. Text and illustrations copyright © 2014 by Lita Judge. Reprinted with permission from Roaring Brook Press, a division of Holtzbrinck Publishing Holdings Limited Partnership. ALL RIGHTS RESERVED.

Page 157: From DID YOU BURP? HOW TO ASK QUESTIONS . . . OR NOT! Text copyright © 2019 by April Pulley Sayre. Illustrations copyright © 2019 by Leeza Hernandez. Used with Permission by Charlesbridge Publishing.

Page 157: From FLIP, FLOAT, FLY: SEEDS ON THE MOVE. Text copyright © JoAnn Early Machen. Illustrations copyright © Pam Paparone. Published in 2008 by Holiday House. Cover used courtesy of Holiday House. All rights reserved.

Page 158: From FLYING FROGS AND WALKING FISH: LEAPING LEMURS, TUMBLING TOADS, JET-PROPELLED JELLYFISH, AND MORE SURPRISING WAYS THAT ANIMALS MOVE. Text copyright © Steve Jenkins and Robin Page. Published in 2016 by Houghton Mifflin Harcourt. Cover used courtesy of Houghton Mifflin Harcourt. All rights reserved.

Page 158: From HANDIMALS: ANIMALS IN ART AND NATURE. Text copyright © 2019 by Silvia Lopez. Illustrations © 2019 by Guido Daniele. Reprinted with permission from Henry Holt Books for Young Readers. ALL RIGHTS RESERVED.

Page 158: From MOVE! Text copyright © Steve Jenkins and Robin Page. Published in 2006 by Holiday House. Cover used courtesy of Holiday House. All rights reserved.

Page 158: From MYSTERIOUS PATTERNS: FINDING FRACTALS IN NATURE. Text copyright © Sarah C. Campbell. Photographs copyright © Sarah C. Campbell and Richard P. Campbell. Published in 2014 by Boyds Mills Press. Cover used by arrangement with Boyds Mills & Kane. All rights reserved.

Page 158: From RODENT RASCALS. Text copyright © Roxie Munro. Published in 2018 by Published in 2018 by Holiday House. Cover used courtesy of Holiday House. All rights reserved.

Page 158: From STRETCH TO THE SUN: FROM A TINY SPROUT TO THE TALLEST TREE ON EARTH. Text copyright © 2018 by Carrie A. Pearson. Illustrations copyright © 2018 by Susan Swan. Used with Permission by Charlesbridge Publishing.

Page 159: From SWIRL BY SWIRL: SPIRALS IN NATURE. Text copyright © Joyce Sidman. Illustrations copyright © Beth Krommes. Published in 2011 by Houghton Mifflin Harcourt. Cover used courtesy of Houghton Mifflin Harcourt. All rights reserved.

Page 159: From TROUT ARE MADE OF TREES. Text copyright © 2008 by April Pulley Sayre. Illustrations copyright © 2008 by Kate Endle. Used with Pemission by Charlesbridge Publishing.

Page 159: From WITH A FRIEND BY YOUR SIDE. Text copyright © Barbara Kerley. Published in 2015 by National Geographic. Cover used courtesy of National Geographic. All rights reserved.

Page 159: From WOLFSNAIL: A BACKYARD PREDATOR. Text and photographs copyright © Sarah C. Campbell. Published in 2008 by Boyds Mills Press. Cover used by arrangement with Boyds Mills & Kane. All rights reserved.

Index

A

active nonfiction. *See also* classification system for nonfiction
  book displays and, 119–120
  classroom book collections and, 37–38
  commercial versus literary nonfiction and, 96–99
  craft moves and, 55
  identifying the best books for a specific purpose, 48–56
  overview, 12*f*, 13, 19–20
  self-selection of texts and, 45–48
  supporting research and, 50–53
  teaching the 5 Kinds of Nonfiction, 40–44
activities. *See also* instruction
  celebrating nonfiction books and, 124–132
  March Madness Nonfiction, 131–132
  list of, 147-151
  planner, 147-151
  reproducibles for, 152-156
Actual Size (Jenkins), 157
Albee, Sarah, 15, 79, 99*f*, 104–105, 133, 151
Alderfer, Jonathan, 19, 41, 147
Animal Bodies Up Close series, 92–94
Aronson, Marc, 12–13, 141
Aston, Dianna Hutts, 18, 69, 72, 102–103, 148, 149, 157
Atkins, Marcie Flinchum, 52, 159
audience, 88
awards for nonfiction, 24–26, 134–135, 151, 156

B

background knowledge, 34, 128–129
Balas, Tali, 3*f*
Bang-Jensen, Valerie, 43–44
Barnett, Mac, 109, 139
Barretta, Gene, 45, 87
Bartle, Sue, 12–13
Beavers (Poliquin), 110
Because of an Acorn (Schafer), 157
Before She Was Harriet (Cline-Ransome), 105, 150
Behind the Scenes Gymnastics (Lawrence), 14
Benjamin Franklin, American Genius (Miller), 44–45
Big & Little (Jenkins), 80
Big Book of WHY (Time for Kids), 15
biographies, 4, 6, 109–110
Bird, Betsy, 19
Birds of a Feather (Roth), 80, 83–84, 111, 126, 139, 149, 157
Bishop, Nic, 85–86, 149
blended nonfiction. *See also* gateway nonfiction; writing styles
  book awards, 25
  overview, 21, 136, 138–144
  role of in literacy development, 143–144
Bober, Tom, 46
Bone by Bone (Levine), 82, 107–108
Bonkers About Beetles (Davey), 79
book clubs, 129–130
book displays, 118–120, 150
Book of Queens, The (Drimmer), 15
book reviews, 135–136, 151
book selection. *See* preferences; text selection for instruction
book talks
  Activity 8.2: Student Book Talks, 122, 151
  book clubs and, 129–130
  introducing nonfiction books to students and, 120–122
  Planning a Book Talk tipsheets, 122, 153–154

book tastings, 123–124

Born in the Wild (Judge), 157

Boy, Were We Wrong About Dinosaurs! (Kudlinski), 35–36, 80

Brown Girl Dreaming (Woodson), 108

browseable nonfiction. *See also* classification system for nonfiction

    Activity 5.2: Text Format in Browseable Books, 66–69, 148

    book displays and, 119–120

    book talks and, 120–122

    classroom book collections and, 37–38

    commercial versus literary nonfiction and, 96–99

    craft moves and, 54*t*

    identifying the best books for a specific purpose, 48–56

    overview, 12*f*, 13, 14–15

    self-selection of texts and, 45–48

    supporting research and, 50–53

    teaching the 5 Kinds of Nonfiction, 40–44

    text features and, 62

    text format and, 66–69

Bugged (Albee), 79

Burleigh, Robert, 110

Burnie, David, 41, 147

Burns, Loree Griffin, 16, 50

Butterflies (Simon), 17

Butterfly Is Patient, A (Aston), 18, 102–103, 149

C

Campbell, Sarah C., 158, 159

Can an Aardvark Bark? (Stewart), 88

Capote, Truman, 16

Cappiello, Mary Ann, 12–13

carefully chosen point of view craft move. *See also* craft moves

Activity 4.3: Nonfiction Appreciation and Examination, 57–59, 147

Activity 7.3: Exploring Point of View in Nonfiction, 111–112, 150

Activity 7.4: Experimenting with Voice and Point of View, 113–116, 150

overview, 54*t*, 107–116

carefully chosen text structure craft move, 54*t*. *See also* craft moves; text structure

Carson, Mary Kay, 7, 20, 82, 132, 149

Castaldo, Nancy F., 140, 142

Category Feature Cards

    book tastings and, 123–124

    complete, 152

    teaching the 5 Kinds of Nonfiction, 41–42, 43

Cause & Effect text structure, 80. *See also* text structure

celebrating nonfiction books, 124–132. *See also* book clubs; March Madness Nonfiction; read-alouds

Chain Reaction text structure, 87. *See also* text structure

choice. *See also* preferences

    Activity 8.1: Creating Nonfiction Book Displays, 120, 150

    Activity 8.2: Student Book Talks, 122, 151

    preview stacks and, 122–123

    self-selection of texts and, 45–48

Christian, Peggy, 105, 150, 158

Chronological Sequence text structure, 6, 79. *See also* text structure

City Hawk (McCarthy), 41, 147

classification system for nonfiction. *See also* active nonfiction; browseable nonfiction; expository literature nonfiction; narrative nonfiction; organization systems for texts; traditional nonfiction

classification system for nonfiction, *continued*

  blended nonfiction and, 138–144

  categories of, 12–20

  classroom book collections and, 37–38

  commercial versus literary nonfiction and, 96–99

  identifying the best books for a specific purpose, 48–56

  introducing nonfiction books to students and, 118–124

  libraries and, 1–2

  overview, 11–13, 20–21

  self-selection of texts and, 45–48

  teaching the 5 Kinds of Nonfiction, 40–44

  understanding the 5 Kinds of Nonfiction and, 44–45

#classroombookaday, 124–125

classroom collections. *See also* libraries

  Activity 8.1: Creating Nonfiction Book Displays, 120, 150

  compared to libraries, 11

  introducing nonfiction books to students and, 118–124

  list of suggested books for reading aloud, 157–159

  obtaining books for, 145

  overview, 37–38

  preview stacks and, 122–123

  student preferences and, 29–31

Cline-Ransome, Lesa, 6, 105, 130*f*, 150

Clinton, Chelsea, 80

Code This! (Szymanski), 19

collections, classroom. *See* classroom collections

commercial nonfiction, 96–99. *See also* active nonfiction; browseable nonfiction

Common Core State Standards, 4, 98

Compare & Contrast text structure, 80, 87, 88. *See also* text structure

compelling beginnings craft move, 54*t*

complex texts. *See also* expository nonfiction

  evaluating, 35–36

  patterns in text and, 72–74

  understanding, 34–35

comprehension

  complex texts and, 34–35

  patterns in text and, 72–74

conferences with students, 28–29

content knowledge, building, 32–34

conversations in the classroom

  book clubs and, 129–130

  book talks and, 120–122, 129–130, 151, 153–154

  read-alouds and, 128–129

Cook, Deanna F., 20

Cooking Class Global Feast! (Cook), 20

Coral Reefs (Gibbons), 14

Cowley, Joy, 7–9, 85–86, 147, 149

craft, nonfiction. *See* nonfiction craft

craft moves, 53–116. *See also* carefully chosen point of view craft move; informational writing; interruption construction; rich, engaging language craft move; strong voice craft move; text features; text format; text scaffolding; text structure; writing

curiosity, 32–34

Cusolito, Michelle, 108, 111, 133, 151

Cute as an Axolotl (Keating), 128, 157

D

Danneberg, Julie, 119

Davey, Owen, 79, 85–86, 149

Davies, Nicola, 79, 107, 158

Daylight Starlight Wildlife (Minor), 80, 157

Day You Begin, The (Woodson), 119

Deadliest Creature in the World, The (Guiberson), 110, 116, 150

De Amicis, Giulia, 15

Dear America series, 4

Death Eaters (Halls), 74, 133, 148, 151

Denise, Anika Aldamuy, 16

Description text structure, 79. *See also* text
    structure

development, literacy, 143–144

Dewey, Melvil, 1

Dewey Decimal System, 1–2

diagrams in text, 62. *See also* text features

Diaz, Abi, 40

DiCamillo, Kate, 96

Did You Burp? (Sayre), 157

Dinosaurs by the Numbers (Jenkins), 111, 150

Doeden, Matt, 14

Dog Days of History (Albee), 133, 151

Doiron, Ray, 30

Dorling Kindersley Eyewitness Books series. *See*
    Eyewitness Books series

Do Sharks Glow in the Dark? . . .
    and Other Shark-tastic Questions
    (Carson), 82, 149

Drimmer, Stephanie Warren, 15, 46

Duprat, Guillaume, 15, 133, 151

E

Earth (Guiberson), 80, 90

educator preferences. *See* preferences

Egg Is Quiet, An (Aston), 69, 72, 126, 148, 157

Ehlert, Lois, 108, 111, 150

ELA lessons. *See* instruction

Emmett, Jennifer, 15

engagement, 32–34, 45–48. *See also* interests of
    students

engaging language. *See* rich, engaging language
    craft move

English language learners, 33–34

Enslow Animal Bodies Up Close series, 149

Enslow Zoom in on Animals series, 63, 148

evaluating nonfiction books
    Activity 8.3: Nonfiction Smackdown!
        Evaluating and Comparing Two Books,
        132–133, 151, 155
    Activity 8.4: Sibert Smackdown! Selecting an
        Award Winner, 134–135, 151, 156
    Activity 8.5: Real Reviews! Writing Book
        Reviews for the School Library Catalog,
        135–136, 151
    overview, 132–136

Exoplanets (Simon), 14

expository literature nonfiction. *See also*
    classification system for nonfiction;
    expository nonfiction; expository writing
    style
    Activity 5.3: Text Format in Expository
        Literature, 71–72, 148
    book displays and, 119–120
    book talks and, 120–122
    commercial versus literary nonfiction and,
        96–99
    craft and, 54*t*, 56–60
    identifying the best books for a specific
        purpose, 48–56
    list of suggested books for reading aloud,
        157–159
    obtaining and finding books, 145–146
    overview, 12*f*, 13, 17–19
    self-selection of texts and, 45–48
    supporting research and, 50–53
    teaching the 5 Kinds of Nonfiction, 40–44
    text features and, 62

expository nonfiction. *See also* expository
    literature nonfiction; expository writing
    style
    Activity 1.1: Comparing Narrative and
        Expository Nonfiction, 7–9, 147

expository nonfiction, *continued*
    classroom book collections and, 37–38
    complex texts and, 34–36
    craft and, 56–60
    instruction and, 31–37
    overview, 5–9
expository writing style. *See also* expository
    nonfiction; writing styles
    classification system for nonfiction and, 13
    educator preferences and, 23–27
    preferences and, 23–31
    student preferences and, 27–31
Eye Spy (Duprat), 15, 133, 151
Eyewitness Books: Birds (Burnie), 41, 147
Eyewitness Books series, 14–15, 66
Eyewitness Books: Whales (Papastavrou),
    66–69, 148

F

Family Literacy Nights, 124
Fanatical About Frogs (Davey), 85–86, 149
Feathered Dinosaurs (Guiberson), 90
Feathers (Stewart), 41, 147
fiction texts
    classification systems in libraries and, 1–2
    informational fiction, 4, 109-110, 116
    organization systems for, 11
    overview, 1
    patterns in, 62
First Day Jitters (Danneberg), 119
first-person narration. *See also* carefully chosen
    point of view craft move
    Activity 7.3: Exploring Point of View in
        Nonfiction, 111–112, 150
    Activity 7.4: Experimenting with Voice and
        Point of View, 113–116, 150
    overview, 108–110
First Read Clubs, 130

Fishman, Seth, 79, 158
5 Kinds of Nonfiction classification system. *See
    also* active nonfiction; blended nonfiction;
    browseable nonfiction; classification
    system for nonfiction; expository
    literature nonfiction; narrative nonfiction;
    traditional nonfiction
    applying, 44–56
    commercial versus literary nonfiction and,
        96–99
    introducing nonfiction books to students
        and, 118–124
    literacy development and, 143–144
    overview, 136
    teaching, 40–44
Fleming, Candace, 67–69, 101–102, 105, 143,
    148, 150, 158
Flip, Float, Fly (Macken), 157
Flying Deep (Cusolito), 108, 111, 133, 151
Flying Frogs and Walking Fish (Jenkins and
    Page), 127–128, 158
Follett Destiny® Library Manager™, 29
Fountas & Pinnell Literacy Continuum, The
    (Fountas and Pinnell), 98
Frank, Sarah, 7, 14
Frog Book, The (Jenkins), 79
Frog or Toad? How Do You Know? (Stewart),
    7–9, 85–86, 147, 149
Frogs (Bishop), 85–86, 149
Frog Song (Guiberson), 85–86, 104, 105, 149,
    150, 158
From Striving to Thriving (Harvey and Ward),
    22, 118
Fuse #8 Production, A (blog), 19

G

Galbraith, Kathryn O., 105, 150, 158
Game Changers (Cline-Ransome), 6

gateway nonfiction, 21, 140, 141–143. *See also* blended nonfiction

Giant Squid (Fleming), 67–69, 101–102, 105, 140, 143, 148, 150, 158

Gibbons, Gail, 11, 14

Girls with Guts (Gonzales), 154

glossary, 62. *See also* text features

Golden Retrievers (Frank), 7, 14

Gonzales, Debbie, 154

Goodnight, Moon (Brown), 139

Great Monkey Rescue, The (Markle), 80, 140, 142

Greenberg, Jan, 6, 16

Guiberson, Brenda Z., 78, 80, 85–86, 90, 104, 105, 110, 116, 149, 150, 158

Guillain, Charlotte, 158

Guinness World Records books, 6–7, 15

H

Hair-Raising Hairstyles That Make a Statement (Rissman), 20

Hale, Christy, 159

Halls, Kelly Milner, 74, 132, 133, 148, 151

Handimals (Lopez), 158

Harvey, Stephanie, 22, 118

Hatch! (Munro), 82

headings, 62. *See also* text features

Hedy Lamarr's Double Life (Wallmark), 76, 148

Heise, Jillian, 124–125

Heos, Bridget, 110

Hey, Kiddo (Krosoczka), 108

Hey, Water (Portis), 110

Hidden Life of a Toad, The (Weschler), 85–86, 149

high-stakes testing, 36–37

historical fiction, 4

Homes in the Wild (Judge), 18, 81

How to Be an Elephant (Roy), 140, 142

How to Clean a Hippopotamus (Jenkins and Page), 70, 72, 148

How to Swallow a Pig (Jenkins and Page), 79, 158

Hundred Billion Trillion Stars, A (Fishman), 79, 158

Hunt, Jonathan, 141

I

I, Fly (Heos), 110

I Am Rosa Parks (Meltzer), 110

Ick! Delightfully Disgusting Animal Dinners, Dwellings, and Defenses (Stewart), 65f

If I Built a School (Van Dusen), 119

If Sharks Disappeared (Williams), 80

If You Decide to Go to the Moon (McNulty), 111, 150

If You Find a Rock (Christian), 105, 150, 158

If You Hopped Like a Frog (Schwartz), 80, 83–84, 105, 111, 149, 150, 158

Igniting a Passion for Reading (Layne), 130

Ignotofsky, Rachel, 18

illustrations in text, 62. *See also* text features

Important Thing About Margaret Wise Brown, The (Barnett), 109, 139

inclusivity in nonfiction titles, 13

independent reading, 45–48, 118–120

index, 62. *See also* text features

informational fiction, 4, 109-110, 116

informational text, definition, 3–4

informational writing. *See also* writing
  nonfiction craft and, 53–116
  supporting with the 5 Kinds of Nonfiction, 53–56
  use of term, 4

innovative format craft move, 54t

instruction. *See also* activities; text selection for instruction

instruction, *continued*
  activity planner for, 147–151
  celebrating nonfiction books and, 124–132
  evaluating nonfiction books, 132–136
  expository nonfiction and, 31–37
  identifying the best books for a specific
    purpose, 48–56
  introducing nonfiction books to students
    and, 118–124
  nonfiction craft and, 53–116
  teaching the 5 Kinds of Nonfiction, 40–44
  text features and, 63–65
interactive texts. *See* active nonfiction
interests of students. *See also* engagement;
    preferences
  book talks and, 120–122
  book tastings and, 123–124
  commercial versus literary nonfiction and,
    96–99
  expository nonfiction and, 32–34
  gateway nonfiction and, 141–143
  identifying the best books for a specific
    purpose, 48–56
  introducing nonfiction books to students
    and, 118–124
  preview stacks and, 122–123
  self-selection of texts and, 45–48
interruption construction, 72–74, 148
  Activity 5.4: Interruption Construction
    Treasure Hunt, 74
invented dialogue in informational fiction, 4, 110
Itch! (Sanchez), 73, 100–101

J

Jarrow, Gail, 6, 16
Jenkins, Steve, 70, 71, 72, 79, 80, 81, 82, 89,
    90–92, 93, 111, 127–128, 132, 148, 149,
    150, 157, 158

Jenson-Elliott, Cindy, 60, 159
Joan Proctor, Dragon Doctor (Valdez), 16
Johnson, Rebecca L., 140, 142
Jordan, Sandra, 6, 16
Judge, Lita, 18, 81, 157

K

Karl's New Beak (Nargi), 16
Keating, Jess, 69, 81, 102–103, 128, 149, 157
Kerley, Barbara, 119, 159
Kirkland, Traci, 10
knowledge, content, 32–34
Korman, Gordon, 96
Krosoczka, Jarrett, 108
Kudlinski, Kathleen, 35–36, 80

L

Ladder text structure, 86–87. *See also* text
    structure
LaMothe, Matt, 81, 111, 119, 150
language. *See* rich, engaging language craft move
Lawrence, Blythe, 14
Layne, Steven, 130
Let's Read and Find Out series, 63, 148
Levine, Sara, 82, 107–108
librarians in schools. *See also* libraries
  benefits of having, 11
  No Child Left Behind Act of 2001 and, 17
  student preferences and, 29
libraries. *See also* classroom collections;
    librarians in schools
  Activity 8.1: Creating Nonfiction Book
    Displays, 120, 150
  Activity 8.5: Real Reviews! Writing Book
    Reviews for the School Library Catalog,
    135–136, 151
  benefits of having, 11
  book displays and, 118–120
  book tastings and, 123–124

classification systems in, 1–2

commercial versus literary nonfiction and, 97

compared to classroom collection, 11

informational text and, 3–4

list of suggested books for reading aloud, 157–159

No Child Left Behind Act of 2001 and, 17

obtaining books for, 145

student preferences and, 29–31

Lincoln and Kennedy (Barretta), 87

List text structure, 81, 89–90. *See also* text structure

literacy development, 143–144

literary nonfiction, 96–99. *See also* expository literature nonfiction; narrative nonfiction

Look at Me! (Jenkins), 81

Lopez, Silvia, 158

Lowery, Ruth McKoy, 39

M

Macken, JoAnn Early, 157

Made for Each Other (Patent), 133, 151

made-up characters in informational fiction, 4, 110, 116

Magic School Bus series, 4

Mama Built a Little Nest (Ward), 69, 71, 148, 158

Many (Davies), 79, 158

maps in text, 62. *See also* text features

March Madness Nonfiction, 131–132

Mario and the Hole in the Sky (Rusch), 76, 148

Markle, Sandra, 18, 73, 80, 92–94, 121, 132, 133, 140, 142, 149, 151

Masiello, Ralph, 20

Masters of Disguise (Johnson), 140, 142

McAnulty, Stacey, 110, 116, 150

McCarthy, Megan, 41, 147

McLean, Kristen, 20

McNulty, Faith, 111, 150

Meltzer, Brad, 110

mentor texts

expository literature nonfiction as, 18

identifying the best books for a specific purpose, 49

informational writing and, 53

overview, 21

text structure and, 90–94

writing expository nonfiction and, 36

Mesmerized (Rockliff), 80

Messner, Kate, 18, 87

Miller, Brandon Marie, 44–45

Minor, Wendell, 80, 157

modeling, 34–35, 53–54

Monster Trucks (Doeden), 14

Montgomery, Heather L., 109

Moody, Shelley, 131

Move! (Jenkins and Page), 71, 158

Munro, Roxie, 80, 82, 87, 158

Mysterious Patterns (Campbell), 158

N

Nargi, Lela, 16

narrative nonfiction. *See also* classification system for nonfiction; writing styles

Activity 1.1: Comparing Narrative and Expository Nonfiction, 7–9, 147

book displays and, 119–120

classroom book collections and, 37–38

commercial versus literary nonfiction and, 96–99

craft moves and, 54*t*, 56–60

educator preferences and, 23–27

identifying the best books for a specific purpose, 48–56

list of suggested books for reading aloud, 157–159

narrative nonfiction, *continued*

    obtaining and finding books, 145–146

    overview, 5–7, 12*f*, 13, 16

    patterns in, 62

    preferences and, 23–31

    self-selection of texts and, 45–48

    student preferences and, 27–31

    supporting research and, 50–53

    teaching the 5 Kinds of Nonfiction, 40–44

National Geographic Kids Bird Guide of North America (Alderfer), 19, 41, 147

National Geographic Readers series, 63, 148

Neighborhood Sharks (Roy), 140, 142

Never Smile at a Monkey (Jenkins), 80, 89

Newman, Patricia, 3*f*

Next President, The (Messner), 18, 87

No Child Left Behind Act of 2001, 2–3, 17

nonfiction craft, 53–116

nonfiction in general. *See also* 5 Kinds of Nonfiction classification system; classification system for nonfiction

    Activity 1.1: Comparing Narrative and Expository Nonfiction, 7–9, 147

    classification systems in libraries and, 1–2

    craft and, 56–116

    informational text, 3–4

    nonfiction writing styles and, 5–7

    overview, 1

    patterns in, 62–94

Nonfiction Smackdown! recording sheet, 133, 151

North America (Albee), 15, 99*f*

Now & Ben (Barretta), 45

O

Ocean (Weiss and De Amicis), 15

One Proud Penny (Siegel), 110

One World, One Day (Kerley), 119

organization systems for texts, 11–13. *See also* classification system for nonfiction

Osborne, Mary Pope, 96

Otis and Will Discover the Deep (Rosenstock), 133, 151

Oxford English Dictionary (ND), 17

P

pacing, 6

Page, Robin, 70, 71, 72, 79, 82, 90–92, 93, 127, 128, 148, 149, 158

Papastavrou, Vassili, 66–69, 148

Paradis, Judi, 132–133

Park, Linda Sue, 99–100

Patent, Dorothy Hinshaw, 133, 151

patterns in text

    Activity 4.3: Nonfiction Appreciation and Examination, 57–59, 147

    Activity 5.1: Text Feature Posters, 63–64. 148

    Activity 5.2: Text Format in Browseable Books, 66–69, 148

    Activity 5.3: Text Format in Expository Literature, 71–72, 148

    Activity 5.4: Interruption Construction Treasure Hunt, 74, 148

    Activity 5.5: Text Scaffolding Treasure Hunt, 76–77, 148

    Activity 6.1: Introducing Text Structures with Q& A, 82–84, 149

    Activity 6.2: Same Topic, Different Structures, 85–86, 149

    Activity 6.3: Experimenting with Text Structures, 90–92, 149

    Activity 6.4: Same Text Structure, New Topic, 92–94, 149

    interruption construction, 72–74

    overview, 62

text features and, 62–65

text format and, 65–72

text scaffolding and, 75–77

text structure, 78-94

Pearson, Carrie A., 111, 158

Penguins (Simon), 41, 147

photos in text, 62. *See also* text features

Picone, Kristen, 41, 51

picture book biographies, 4

Pink Is for Blobfish (Keating), 69, 81, 102–103, 149

Pipsqueaks, Slowpokes, and Stinkers (Stewart), 127, 158

Place for Frogs, A (Stewart), 85–86, 149

Planning a Book Talk tipsheets, 122, 153–154

Planting Stories (Denise), 16

Planting the Wild Garden (Galbraith), 105, 150, 158

Poet (Tate), 111, 112*f*, 150

point of view. *See* carefully chosen point of view craft move

Poison (Albee), 104–105

Poliquin, Rachel, 110

Portis, Antoinette, 110

preferences. *See also* choice; interests of students

    book tastings and, 123–124

    classroom book collections and, 37–38

    commercial versus literary nonfiction and, 96–99

    educator preferences, 23–27

    gateway nonfiction and, 141–143

    identifying the best books for a specific purpose, 48–56

    of most educators, 23–27

    overview, 27–31

    read-alouds and, 125

    self-selection of texts and, 45–48

    writing styles and, 23–31

preview stacks, 122–123

prior knowledge. *See* background knowledge

Problem-Solution text structure, 80. *See also* text structure

procedural writing, 49, 55. *See also* writing

Progress in International Reading Literacy Study (PIRLS), 37

pseudo-narratives, 110, 116

purpose for writing, 88

Q

Question & Answer text structure, 81, 82–84, 149. *See also* text structure

R

Ralph Masiello's Alien Drawing Book (Masiello), 20

read-alouds

    #classroombookaday, 124-125

    Jillian Heise, 124

    complex texts and, 34–36

    encouraging student responses, 128–129

    list of suggested books for, 157–159

    locating books for, 126–127

    overview, 124–129

    tips and tricks for reading nonfiction aloud, 127–128

    using think-alouds to examine text features and, 64–65

reading conferences, 28–29

Red-Eyed Tree Frog (Cowley), 7–9, 85–86, 147, 149

research, supporting, 14-18, 50–53

reviews, book, 135–136, 151

Rex, Adam, 119

rhythm, 99–100. *See also* strong voice craft move

rich, engaging language craft move, 54*t*, 103–107, 150. *See also* craft moves

Activity 4.3: Nonfiction Appreciation and Examination, 57–59, 147

Activity 7.2: Appreciating Rich Language in Nonfiction, 105-107, 150

Rissman, Rebecca, 20

Rivers and Streams (Sills), 14

Robert F. Sibert Informational Book Medal, 134–135, 151, 156

Rockliff, Mara, 80

Rodent Rascals (Munro), 80, 87, 158

Rosenblatt, Louise, 26–27, 48–49

Rosenstock, Barb, 133, 151

Roth, Susan L., 80, 83–84, 111, 126, 139, 149, 157

Rotten! (Sanchez), 18, 133, 151

Roy, Katherine, 140, 142

Runaway Bunny (Brown), 139

Rusch, Elizabeth, 76, 148

S

Sanchez, Anita, 18, 73, 100–101, 133, 151

satisfying endings craft move, 54*t*

Sayre, April Pulley, 79, 105, 128, 132, 150, 157, 159

Schafer, Lola M., 157

Scholastic What If You Had series, 92–94, 149

School's First Day of School (Rex), 119

Schwartz, David M., 71, 80, 83–84, 105, 111, 148, 149, 150, 158

Scraps Book, The (Ehlert), 108, 111, 150

Sea Otter Heroes (Newman), 2*f*

second-person narration. *See also* carefully chosen point of view craft move

Activity 7.3: Exploring Point of View in Nonfiction, 111–112, 150

Activity 7.4: Experimenting with Voice and Point of View, 113–116, 150

overview, 107–108

Seed Is the Start, A (Stewart), 133, 151

Seeds Move (Page), 133, 151

self-selection of texts, 45–48, 50–51

Sequence text structure, 79, 88. *See also* text structure

She Persisted (Clinton), 80

Sibert Smackdown activity, 134–135, 156

Sidman, Joyce, 86–87, 159

Sills, Cathryn, 14

Simon, Seymour, 11, 14, 17, 41, 46, 147

small group work

book clubs and, 129–130

evaluating complex texts and, 36

teaching the 5 Kinds of Nonfiction, 40–44

Sniffer Dogs (Castaldo), 140, 142

Snowy Owl Invasion! (Markle), 73, 140, 142

Solving the Puzzle Under the Sea (Burleigh), 110

Something Rotten (Montgomery), 109

Sorell, Traci, 7, 79, 103, 105, 150, 159

Spooked! (Jarrow), 6, 16

Squirrels Leap, Squirrels Sleep (Sayre), 105, 150

stacks, preview. *See* preview stacks

standardized test preparation, 36–37

standards, 36–37, 98. *See also* craft moves

STEM-themed books, 4, 17

Stewart, Melissa, 7–9, 41, 64–65, 65*f*, 85–86, 88, 92–94, 127, 132, 133, 147, 149, 151, 158

storytelling in nonfiction, 5-6, 7-9, 16. *See also* narrative nonfiction.

Street Beneath My Feet, The (Guillain), 158

Stretch to the Sun (Pearson), 111, 158

strong voice craft move, 54*t*, 99–103, 149. *See also* craft moves

Activity 4.3: Nonfiction Appreciation and Examination, 57–59, 147

Activity 7.1: Exploring Voice in Nonfiction, 102–103, 149

Activity 7.4: Experimenting with Voice and Point of View, 113–116, 150

student interest. *See* interests of students

student preferences. *See* preferences

Sun (McAnulty), 110, 116, 150

Super Gear (Swanson), 75–76

survey books, 11. *See also* traditional nonfiction

Swanson, Jennifer, 75–76

Swirl by Swirl (Sidman), 86–87, 159

Szymanski, Jennifer, 19

T

table of contents, 62. *See also* text features

Tarshis, Lauren, 96

Tate, Don, 111, 112*f*, 150

teacher preferences. *See* preferences

teaching the 5 Kinds of Nonfiction. *See* instruction

test preparation, 36–37

text features, 62–65, 148

Activity 4.3: Nonfiction Appreciation and Examination, 57–59, 147

Activity 5.1: Text Feature Posters. 63-64, 148

text features craft move, 54*t*, 56

text feature walk strategy, 63

text format. *See also* craft moves

Activity 5.2: Text Format in Browseable Books, 66–69, 148

Activity 5.3: Text Format in Expository Literature, 71–72, 148

overview, 56

patterns in text and, 62–94

text patterns. *See* patterns in text

text scaffolding, 75–77, 148.

Activity 5.5: Text Scaffolding Treasure Hunt, 76–77, 148

text selection for instruction. *See also* instruction

gateway nonfiction and, 141–143

identifying the best books for a specific purpose, 48–56

list of suggested books for reading aloud, 157–159

obtaining and finding books, 145–146

overview, 31–37

read-alouds and, 126–127

self-selection of texts and, 45–48, 50–51

student preferences and, 30–31

supporting research and, 14-18, 50–53

text structure. *See also* carefully chosen text structure craft move; Cause & Effect text structure; Chronological Sequence text structure; Compare & Contrast text structure; craft moves; Description text structure; List text structure; Problem-Solution text structure; Question & Answer text structure; Sequence text structure

active nonfiction and, 19

Activity 4.3: Nonfiction Appreciation and Examination, 57–59, 147

Activity 1.1: Comparing Narrative and Expository Nonfiction, 7–9, 147

Activity 6.1: Introducing Text Structures with Q&A, 82–84, 149

Activity 6.2: Same Topic, Different Text Structures, 85–86, 149

Activity 6.3: Experimenting with Text Structure, 90–92, 149

Activity 6.4: Same Text Structure, New Topic, 92–94, 149

browseable nonfiction and, 15

text structure, *continued*

  expository literature nonfiction and, 17–18

  narrative nonfiction and, 16

  overview, 56, 79–86

  traditional nonfiction and, 13

  in writing, 86–94

think-alouds, 64–65

third-person narration. *See also* carefully chosen
    point of view craft move

  Activity 7.3: Exploring Point of View in
    Nonfiction, 111–112, 150

  Activity 7.4: Experimenting with Voice and
    Point of View, 113–116, 150

This Is How We Do It (LaMothe), 81, 111,
    119, 150

tier 3 vocabulary words, 33–34

Time for Kids Big Book of Why, 6–7

Tiny Creatures (Davies), 107

tone, 100

Tovani, Cris, 48–49

traditional nonfiction. *See also* 5 Kinds
    of Nonfiction classification system;
    classification system for nonfiction; survey
    books

  book displays and, 119–120

  book talks and, 120–122

  classroom book collections and, 37–38

  commercial versus literary nonfiction and, 97

  craft moves and, 55

  identifying the best books for a specific
    purpose, 48–56

  overview, 12*f*, 13–14

  self-selection of texts and, 45–48

  supporting research and, 50–53

  teaching the 5 Kinds of Nonfiction, 40–44

  text features and, 62

Transactional Theory of Reading, 26–27

Trout Are Made of Trees (Sayre), 79, 126, 159

Two Brothers, Four Hands (Greenberg and
    Jordan), 6, 16

U

Ultimate Weather-pedia (Drimmer), 46

Uncommon Corps, 12–13

V

Valdez, Patricia, 16

Van Dusen, Chris, 119

Venkatraman, Padma, 96

Verbs, strong/vivid, 58, 71, 104, 105-107, 120,
    156

  Activity 4.3: Nonfiction Appreciation and
    Examination, 57–59, 147

  Activity 7.2: Appreciating Rich Language in
    Nonfiction, 105-107

Vincent, Jen, 61, 95

vocabulary, 33–34

voice. *See* strong voice craft move

W

Wait, Rest, Pause (Atkins), 52, 56, 159

Walker, Sally M., 132

Wallmark, Laurie, 76, 148

Warbler Wave (Sayre), 128, 159

Ward, Annie, 22

Ward, Jennifer, 69, 71, 118, 148, 158

Water Land (Hale), 159

We Are Grateful (Sorell), 7, 18, 79, 103, 105,
    150, 159

Weather (Simon), 46

Weeds Find a Way (Jenson-Elliott), 60, 159

Weschler, Doug, 85–86, 149

What Do You Do with a Tail Like This?
    (Jenkins and Page), 82, 90–92, 93, 149

What If You Had Animal Ears (Markle), 121

What If You Had Animal Eyes? (Markle), 133,
    151

What If You Had series, 92–94, 149

What If You Had T. rex Teeth? And Other Dinosaur Parts (Markle), 18

When Lunch Fights Back (Johnson), 140, 142

Where in the Wild? (Schwartz), 71, 148

Wildlife Ranger Action Guide (Carson), 7, 20

Williams, Lily, 80

With a Friend by Your Side (Kerley), 159

Wolfsnail (Campbell), 159

Women in Art (Ignotofsky), 18

Woodson, Jacqueline, 96, 108, 119

word choice, 99–106, 113-116. *See also* rich, engaging language craft move, strong voice craft move

    Activity 4.3: Nonfiction Appreciation and Examination, 57–59, 147

    Activity 7.1: Exploring Voice in Nonfiction, 102–103, 149

    Activity 7.2: Appreciating Rich Language in Nonfiction, 105-107, 150

    Activity 7.4: Experimenting with Voice and Point of View, 113–116, 150

World Is Waiting for You, The (Kerley), 159

writing. *See also* craft moves; informational writing; procedural writing; writing styles

    identifying the best books for a specific purpose, 49

    instruction and, 36

    nonfiction craft and, 53–116

    supporting with the 5 Kinds of Nonfiction, 53–56

    text structure and, 86–94

writing styles. *See also* expository nonfiction; narrative nonfiction; writing

    Activity 1.1: Comparing Narrative and Expository Nonfiction, 7–9, 147

    classroom book collections and, 37–38

    complex texts and, 34–36

    overview, 5–7

    preferences and, 23–31

writing workshops, 18

Y

Young, Terrence Jr., 137

Young Terrell, 19

You're Invited to a Moth Ball (Burns), 16

Z

Zarnowski, Myra, 12–13

Zombie Makers (Johnson), 140, 142

Zoom in on Bees (Stewart), 64–65

Made in United States
Troutdale, OR
04/26/2024

19470704R00135